W9-DIM-010

A Manager's Guide to Conducting Terminations

A Manager's Guide to Conducting Terminations

Minimizing Emotional Stress and Legal Risks

Donald H. Sweet

Lexington Books
D.C. Heath and Company/Lexington, Massachusetts/Toronto

Library of Congress Cataloging-in-Publication Data

Sweet, Donald H.
  A manager's guide to conducting terminations.

  1. Employees, Dismissal of. I. Title.
HF5549.5.D55S93 1988   658.3'13   87–45578
ISBN 0–669–16750–9 (alk. paper)

Published simultaneously in Canada
Printed in the United States of America
International Standard Book Number: 0–669–16750–9
Library of Congress Catalog Card Number 87–45578

The paper used in this publication meets the minimum requirements of American National
Standard for Information Sciences—Permanence of Paper for Printed Library Materials, ANSI
Z39.48–1984. ∞™

88 89 90 91 92 8 7 6 5 4 3 2 1

Contents

Foreword

James J. Gallagher, Ph.D.
Chairman, J. J. Gallagher Associates
Corporate Career Consultants
New York City

The shadow of The Turk looms over corporate offices these days as it does over locker rooms of professional football teams. Executives with steady jobs, who work hard and demonstrate loyalty to employers, are no better off than linebackers and right guards on the day of "the cut." Football players at least depersonalize the bearer of the message that a player isn't on the team. They call that person The Turk. Business executives currently can't be sure whether they will be the bearer or the hearer of The Turk's message.

With job security fast becoming part of the great American myth, and managers uncertain of how to handle job insecurity—their own and their workers'—there is an enormous need for this clear and readable book on terminations.

Like it or not, firing people and getting fired are now part of every manager's job description. In fact, two decades of repairing the damages done to people and organizations by terminations convinced me that a qualification for top management had to include being fired at least once. Until now, personal experience was the only way to guarantee the level of rational compassion needed to fire people well.

Bringing light to this dark side of a manager's job, Don Sweet wrote the book I wish had been available twenty years ago. It took those years of his experience to construct answers to the often unspoken questions that bring cold sweats and sometimes simply immobilize the executive faced with the fact of firing.

Without the wisdom of such experience, executives are disturbed by a range of emotional and practical problems. The work of outplacement consultants suggests a set of four common concerns that are addressed in the chapters that follow:

1. Will this termination *hurt?* Critics notwithstanding, corporations are not insensitive to human issues, and the managers who make up corporations do have real problems inflicting career damage on a colleague. This

is particularly true when company-wide cutbacks are the cause for firing and "villains" are nowhere identified. But even when the case originates in poor performance, I have never met a manager vengeful enough to want to harm an employee.

Workplace Violence

2. Will the employee *hate* the company, and hate me as well? Managers know it is bad business to create enemies. Former employees are most likely to be hired by competitors, suppliers, or customers. Likewise, business relationships spill over to personal life. A manager doesn't want to face the anger of the person just fired when they meet at worship services, the golf club, or a trade association.

3. Will the employee recover from firing, or decide to *hide?* The fired executive who views termination as the end of a career, and never really gets back on track, is a threat to all concerned: the company, the manager, the remaining staff, and most of all, to him- or herself. Nobody wants to view a disaster, especially one we all feel vulnerable about.

4. Will the terminated person come back to *haunt* us? Poorly done terminations have a way of never going away. Maybe the boss wasn't really clear in communicating the message that the job is over. Maybe the message wasn't—couldn't be—understood. The unfinished termination interferes with two vital agendas: the fired employee needs to get busy in job search; the company and manager need to continue the work of the business.

If a book for business people needs to provide solid, substantive help for the reader, then this book is essential reading for managers across the functions of organization life. With the generous insertion of examples and illustrations of true-to-life situations that all managers face, this serious subject turns out to be an interesting read as well.

Line managers are well advised not to skip the chapter on advice for human resource professionals. It includes valuable experience that the author has earned in a career of working with both human resource and general managers on the problems they both face in hiring and firing.

Practical advice to me means advice that can be put readily into practice. This book brings to mind and answers a number of the questions managers ask most often when preparing for outplacement of a staff member. If the questions sound familiar, or if you believe they could sound familiar the next time you have to terminate an employee, then you need to read further. You could be asking:

- Why is this termination necessary?

- As long as it has to happen, what is fair to the employee in terms of notice, severance, assistance in job search?

— How do I get ready for a termination interview?

— What do I say to the person I'm firing? And what do I have to be careful not to say?

— What do I say to the rest of the staff and to the people who call for references?

— How does the company and the boss avoid being sued for wrongful discharge?

— Is outplacement necessary and worth the cost?

— How can a company avoid the "self-inflicted wound" of termination?

The list could go on. Suffice it to say that after reading practically everything that has been published in the field of termination policy, I know of no single work that informs, instructs, and brings into focus so skillfully what a manager needs to know.

It may be true that information about termination is, happily, not called for every day. But I have never known a low-visibility termination. When it is called for, skill in managing a termination becomes high-priority and needed immediately. This easily read book provides the preparation every manager needs to master ahead of time.

Preface

F or most of my career in personnel since 1949, I have been a student
of career management, the psychology of terminations and, in more
recent years, outplacement. I am continually intrigued that in light of
all the constant publicity about layoffs, restructuring, and other factors causing people to be terminated, so many organizations still take a head-in-the-
sand attitude: "It can't happen here. We are too well managed to have other
than the occasional firing of an incompetent." Unfortunately, this subject of
termination is one that no one wants to talk about or deal with—it's a dirty
subject. Until it's a real and immediate problem, we all tend to turn our
backs on it.

Terminations are here to stay and the future portends more, not less.
Our growing "global" economy will ensure this, with its ever-broadening
competition, ever-growing markets, instantaneous communication, and a
myriad of other factors.

Donald is forty-five years old, married with two children, one a junior
at State U. He has a lovely, caring wife and a nice home in the suburbs.
There are two cars in the garage and a summer cottage in Maine. Donald
has an undergraduate degree in engineering and an MBA in finance. He
works for a well-known computer manufacturer, only his second job since
graduation, and his record of performance with the company has been very
good. Both Donald and his wife are involved in the community and have an
active social life. The American dream? No, not really, because Donald will
be terminated from his job today.

Why Donald? It may be for a variety of reasons. It does not appear to
be incompetence, as attested to by his good performance. It may be that his
company has been acquired and there are redundant jobs in the subsequent
consolidation. It may be that the company has lost a significant portion of
its market share, and survival dictates a staff reduction. It may be that the
company is going to relocate and Donald cannot move for personal reasons.
It may be that Donald's boss just doesn't like him and has decided to move
him out. The point is that the Donalds of the world do lose jobs for reasons

other than nonperformance. Regardless of the rationale for the decision, however, terminating is not easy.

Because there have been and will continue to be more "Donald situations," there is an increased concern and awareness about the termination process in its broadest aspects. Terminations, whether of an individual or a group of individuals, have impact on the organization and society in general. It is imperative that all involved with the people processes in any organization understand better and give more consideration to how terminations are handled. This problem has pervaded every organization, or will, and unfortunately, most are ill prepared to deal with the nuances and subtleties and the emotion and trauma involved. The procedures and processes of terminations and the increasing risk of litigation demand that all the *i*'s be dotted and the *t*'s crossed. The practicing manager and the human resources (HR) manager are truly under the gun: the practicing manager has the real responsibility for terminating; and the HR manager has the administrative responsibility. It is not a question of simply getting rid of the problem, but resolving it in a professional, sensitive and humane manner, and understanding the full impact of the action.

The various case histories in this book should make it a real-world resource. They should be of particular value when a manager is faced with a specific termination situation and may help to define a resolution based on the facts presented. This work will also be an asset in developing training and orientation programs.

Chapter 1, "Terminations—A Management Tool?," provides an overview of the subject and explains why the problem has become more complex and confusing. It discusses some fundamentals of the subject to bring it into a clearer perspective for the practicing manager and the HR manager.

In the second chapter, "The Termination Checklist," the operational aspects are covered in some detail. An understanding of these factors is imperative if terminating is to be professional, humane and sensitive.

Chapter 3, "The Termination Interview," deals with the actual encounter between the manager and the individual being terminated. "How-to" procedures to deal with the emotions, resentment, and disappointment of the terminated employee, as well as specific questions typically raised and suggested responses, are covered in detail. This is the essential chapter around which the rest of the text revolves.

The next chapter, "A Manager's Perspective on the Psychology of Terminations," is the manager's key to understanding the importance of the whole subject. Until managers understand others' reactions, they can't understand theirs. The way to anticipate termination problems is to understand the psychology of its impact. Terminations cannot be done professionally or with the proper degree of sensitivity unless the depth of emotion and trauma that may be evoked by all parties, including themselves, is truly understood.

Several case histories define the hurt and angered resentment that often accompany the termination.

In chapter 5, "Avoiding Termination's Pitfalls," a practicing manager's needs are explored in some detail. The discussion emphasizes that all of one's managerial skills are needed to terminate effectively. It also provides further understanding of the inextricable linkage of the total "people process" in an organization, and of the manager's role.

Chapter 6, "The Human Resources Manager's Role: Control and Training," outlines the need for policies and procedures to define the specific responsibilities of the human resources and the practicing manager in the linkage of terminations—from employment to the exit interview. It also defines the areas that need training attention—not how to structure the needed programs (that's for the training experts), but rather the specifics to be emphasized in order to minimize problems.

The last chapter, "Outplacement—The Newest Employee Benefit," explains in a practical manner what this highly publicized but very misunderstood process offers in benefits for the organization and the individuals involved. The text provides a framework for determining the value of outplacement for an organization, and most importantly, indicates how to select the firm best suited to meet needs.

I have tried with this book, based on firsthand experiences over the years in business, to point out the problem areas for any organization and to suggest some meaningful approaches and solutions for the practicing manager and the human resources manager. No one book or individual could possibly answer all the questions about so complex a subject, but I hope I have made this a text practical enough to provoke some thought, and, I hope, some positive action in many organizations. Neither did I write this book to be placed unopened on the office bookshelf, but rather a book to be read and adapted to the unique termination problems in the reader's own environment.

Above all, I hope it will eliminate or minimize some of those sleepless nights and sweaty palms.

Acknowledgments

No one can write on a subject as complicated as this without the assistance and encouragement of others. Dr. James Gallagher, chairman of J.J. Gallagher Associates, has been of inestimable help, not only in the preparation of this book, but as a professional associate for many years. Many of my bosses and peers over the years have taught me a great deal, and in particular, Robert Gallant, who is no longer with us, but whose wisdom I treasure. Some of the most valuable input has come from the scores of individuals I have had the privilege of working with as they made the transition from one career to another, or from one organization to another. Many have become friends, and I will forever be grateful for what I have learned from our association.

Above all, I must recognize my biggest supporter and most patient critic, my wife, Mary, who has suffered through six books with me.

1
Terminations—A Management Tool?

Your Services Are No Longer Required

It's late Friday afternoon at Random Corporation and the following scenario takes place in the office of the vice-president of sales, Dan. The other individual involved is Fred, eastern region sales manager, forty-eight years old and a ten-year employee.

> *Dan (on the phone):* Fred, please come on down to my office right now.
>
> *Fred:* I was trying to finish up my weekly report so Jane could type it before she leaves for the weekend.
>
> *Dan:* Okay, but no longer than ten minutes—it's 4:30 now.

Fred Arrives

> *Dan:* There's something we need to talk about. . . .
>
> *Fred:* What's that?
>
> *Dan:* You.
>
> *Fred:* Okay; what's up?
>
> *Dan:* No, it's not really okay—I am going to have to *fire* you.
>
> *Fred:* Dan, you must be kidding!
>
> *Dan:* No, it's a fact. You really haven't been producing, and Ed is upset about it.
>
> *Fred:* What about you? You told me in my appraisal last month that I was doing fine, and had a real future here! What about the increase you gave me? I know it was above the average. What about the promises you made when I joined the company?
>
> *Dan:* Look, I think you're good, but Ed has reservations. You know how Ed's mind works, and he is the boss . . . he's like the rest of those guys upstairs.
>
> *Fred:* Yea, but you're my boss—you know I can do the job. What's Ed's gripe? What's the real reason?
>
> *Dan:* Well, he just isn't pleased with the way you handled the Smith Corporation account.
>
> *Fred:* What?! You know what happened there. It wasn't my fault those shipments were late. We straightened that out and they were very pleased. Their president told you that.

Dan: Well, it's more than that. Ed doesn't think your style is right. Remember the Morgan Company—they are one of your key accounts? They wanted a new man to handle them.

Fred: Morgan's never happy, you know that; and as to my style—I've been one of the most successful regional managers in the organization. I brought the region to number one in a year and a half! My appraisal pointed up my success and said my interpersonal relationships are outstanding. My customers love me.

Dan: Well, it's an accomplished fact, and it's irrevocable, so let's get on with it.

Fred: Like hell! I'm not going to sit back and take this. I'm going to see the president and get this straightened out.

Dan: I really can't stop you from doing that, but I think it would be a mistake—he doesn't like to be bothered with things like this, so I don't see any positive value to it. As you know, the decision has been approved through company procedures, so it is irrevocable anyway. Why not turn all your energies to the task at hand?

Fred: That's easy for you to say, you don't have the problem. I'll tell you what I might do; I'll sue. I'm forty-eight years old, you know.

Dan: I would give some real thought to that, Fred. It's a lot of trouble, and big companies can keep you in court forever. Obviously, it's your decision, but I think it's a no-win situation.

Fred: C'mon, don't give me that; there must be a job somewhere in this company. What about the promises made when I came here about careers and the potential to move into general management?

Dan: Before we made the decision, we crossed all those bridges and we were not successful in finding another job that would make sense. So, it's an irrevocable decision—anyway, promises are only promises. Let's proceed with other details.

Fred: All you say is "irrevocable"! Why me? Frank's region has been consistently below quotas for the last two years; and Bob's constantly having trouble with this region, . . . and his drinking. . . ."

Dan: I wouldn't have expected you to agree with the decision, but as your boss, I do have an obligation to communicate it to you and to tell you about some of the procedures involved.

Fred: Remember, when you interviewed me I asked about an employment contract, and you said, "we take care of our people." All your brochures say that. How do I break the news at home? My God, I have two kids in college. You know Bill's graduating, and we're having a party for him tonight.

Dan: I forgot, but face up to it directly; I'm sure your wife will be supportive, and the company is going to help with the transition to your new job . . . the Personnel Department will provide outplacement. You won't have any trouble finding a job. It's a good time to be looking. Look, its a fact, so let's proceed. You can stay for another week, then you have three months' severance coming, plus your vacation pay. I want you to see Betty Goshen in Personnel first thing Monday to iron out the details.

Fred: Betty! Isn't she the girl in the benefits office?

Dan: Yes. She is going to give you outplacement help. She will help with a resumé, and I'm sure she has a list of search firms for your use.

Fred: Can't I have more time? It isn't going to be easy to find another job.

Dan: Look, Fred, you're good, and I'm sure you can find another job. There are lots of ads in the paper and the list of search firms will help.

Fred: I've read that it takes a month of looking for every $10K of salary, and you may not recall, but you just raised me to $85K. I am not going to accept this lying down. This is a most unprofessional approach. I can't believe you are really doing this. I think you are lying to me.

Dan: Well, I'm sorry you feel that way, but as far as I'm concerned, what I said are the facts, and Ed also said he feels we need to spruce up the organization.

Fred: "Spruce up"? What's that supposed to mean?

Dan: Well, uh, . . . uh, . . . we feel we do need some fresh blood . . . some younger people. By the way, don't tell anyone about this. We want to make the transition as smooth as possible. Don't tell your secretary, or it will be all over the place. We may just say you resigned; then everyone will be pacified. I have asked public relations to put together a release to that effect.

Fred: You told me I was being fired. What's this "resignation" ploy? A cover-up? Dan, you must think I'm an idiot—I want to talk this through and work out an equitable arrangement for myself, and if you don't believe me, I'll be back with a lawyer Monday.

Dan: I'd like to give you more time, but it's out of my hands, and policy is policy. I'm sorry, because you're a good guy, but it's all done and is effective as of now. Betty will explain the severance arrangements on Monday. So, let's get on with it, okay? Monday, early. Oh, by the way, we would like to have you break in your replacement. She reports next week. She's very good—it shouldn't take more than a day or two.

Fred: I don't believe you!!!

Dan: Look, I've got to run, it's late and we are going out tonight. Have a nice weekend!

This is purposefully an example of a poor termination, but a perfect example of "let's get this odious task out of the way." In all practicality, Dan may have wanted to get this done so he could have a weekend freed from the anxiety of having to fire Fred on Monday. It also seems obvious that Random Corporation, either through naïveté or neglect, paid little attention to such matters that would allow a dialogue like this to take place. If policies and procedures relative to terminations existed at Random, it seems that no one was following them. It also appears that no one assumed any training or orientation responsibility for managers charged with this task.

The result of this episode was a lawsuit by Fred. His attorney successfully made his case, based on the selection process and promises about careers and future potential; on the comment about fresh blood, which was interpreted as an age discrimination remark; and on Fred's most recent appraisal and salary increase. Random settled out of court and Fred received a substantial award, and is now happily employed with another organization in a responsible sales position.

This example, even though it may appear unrealistic, is unfortunately not that farfetched. It should serve as a warning that the practicing manager, as well as the human resources manager, need to make every effort to thoroughly digest all the information about this emotional and sensitive subject of termination. Doing so will improve the odds that, when you must terminate someone, you will conduct the process in a professional and humane manner which will reflect positively on you and your organization.

Death, Taxes, and Terminations

Death and taxes used to be the only two sure and constant things in life. In recent years, however, termination (or the threat of) has become a third. Terminations are a negative subject and one that no one really likes to deal with. Even the vocabulary used to describe the process makes it unpleasant—*fired, laid off, terminated,* and other jargon such as *canned, chopped.* All of these terms denote something terrible and final.

Fired is probably the word most often used, and yet, in a majority of instances, it is incorrect. *Fired* implies involuntary dismissal for cause (poor performance, violation of rules, and so on). It is the most negative term, and implies incompetence, failure, something wrong. Most people do not lose their job for any of those reasons. In subsequent chapters the total subject of terminations will be discussed relative to all types of reasons for terminations, such as job abolished, reduction in force, politics, and also *fired.* Critical to understanding the reason for an individual leaving an organization is that it almost always has a direct relationship to what type of support, psychological, financial and logistical, they will receive. The subject of termination, like everything else in business, has changed and continues to change dramatically, and the future portends more because of our volatile world economy and the continued merger/acquisition mania and corporate budget cutting and attendant restructuring and reorganization. Not too many years ago, termination was primarily a tool for eliminating incompetency from an organization, but in recent times it has become more and more a management tool for implementing the restructuring, downsizing and re-alignment that is taking place. In today's world of work, there are a number of reasons people are terminated, the more specific ones being:

1. merger or acquisition, which requires organization restructuring and consolidation of the work force;

2. discontinuance of a service or the closing or relocation of a particular facility, where personnel may not be invited to move or cannot relocate due to personal considerations;

3. reduction in a work force, prompted by contract cancellations or a shrinking or disappearing market;

4. expansion, where broader skills required in a growth environment may exceed the capabilities of incumbents;

5. ineffective performance, demonstrated by an inability to fulfill assigned duties.

I Hired You, Now I Have To Fire You

Of all the aspects of terminating an employee, one of the most difficult situations for the manager is terminating an individual he or she hired. That makes an unpleasant task even more odious.

At General Quantum Manufacturing, Carl Rice, the director of customer service, was finally facing up to a problem with Paul King, one of his key employees. Actually, it was a problem that Carl had procrastinated about for quite some time, because Paul was a friend and had been since Carl hired him ten years before. Carl had dragged his feet in spite of the fact that Paul really hadn't been doing the job for several years. Carl, like many other managers, had never given much thought to terminating and such consid-erations as employment at will or the legal implications involved. He had read and heard about them, but it was always someone else's problem. Now he had crossed the bridge, and as distasteful as it might be, something had to be done. After a sleepless night, and with a bad case of sweaty palms, he had to face up to the problem; he could no longer procrastinate on the basis of the friendship. He had thought about every way out, such as arranging a transfer to put Paul with someone else in the organization and let him handle the problem. He had even tried to get the personnel department to develop a plan and have them do the actual termination, but to no avail.

An unusual situation? Absolutely not! Not facing up to a termination is common. Termination is difficult even when the issue is nonperformance. It is always an emotional and traumatic experience both for the manager responsible and for the person being terminated. There are a myriad of reasons and reactions that will be elaborated on in subsequent chapters.

Politics, Not Performance

Although not fully understood, it is a business fact that more people lose jobs *not* because of their "lack of technical competence," but because of all the pitfalls inherent in organizations. Outplacement practitioners, who tend to take a relatively objective and practical view of the business of termination because it is their business, agree that it is seldom incompetence that causes one to be terminated. Along that same line, some hard facts have been noted in *Sacked: Why Good People Get Fired and How to Avoid It*.

> A recent survey of top Human Resource Executives uncovered an interesting result: only 16% of executives fired were fired for "poor performance." There were four main issues examined in the survey—personality, strategy, management philosophy, and role conflict. Of the "good performers" who were fired, 70% were let go because of "relationship" problems, usually with the person's boss.[1]

If not something within the individual's control, the reason for termination is most often the politics of the organization or the politics of a specific situation (*politics,* by this definition, being interpersonal relationships). Outplacement professionals also talk about the fact that "skills competence gets you so far, political competence will get you further!" Politics then, is a euphemism for ineptness at interpersonal skills by either party to a termination.

Performance is often a "beauty-is-in-the-eye-of-the-beholder" concept. In other words, what may be viewed as poor performance at Widget Manufacturing may be perfectly acceptable at Avery Manufacturing. Many people judged to be incompetent or poor performers are often simply a victim of the environment in which they work. A change, however accomplished, may be the most positive factor for both parties. A good analogy may be the baseball player who is batting .220 at San Diego, gets traded to Boston, and ends the year hitting .300 with 100 RBIs. Why? A new boss, new co-workers (i.e. teammates), new environment.

I Just Don't Like You

Lucille was the newly hired director of marketing at Fasmatic Manufacturing Corporation. She took over a rather large staff, including Joan Breen, a senior market analyst who had had a meteoric rise in the Fasmatic organization. Joan was a top-notch performer and obviously still on the way up—a fast-tracker. There were some immediate, subtle signs that Lucille wasn't comfortable with Joan, but Joan attributed them to her newness to the Fasmatic environment. Lucille just had not liked Joan from the first day, however, and this feeling was exacerbated by continual comments made by other employees about Joan's quick mind and excellent marketing skills. Joan found that Lucille increasingly vetoed her best ideas, and critiqued every phase of her job, even rewriting her memos. It was obvious she was waiting for Joan to goof. Joan found it more and more difficult to do her job effectively, and finally asked to discuss the situation with Lucille.

A meeting was set, and Joan asked: "What is wrong? I have never had any trouble in getting the job done before." Lucille's response was quite a shock to Joan. "I'm just not really comfortable and I have a feeling this is not going to work out to our mutual advantage. Maybe you ought to go ahead and look around with my approval." Joan was flabbergasted. "What haven't I done?" she asked. "Can you be more specific? Are there some examples?" Lucille responded, "No; it's just my feeling that this won't work, and I want to be fair to you."

Even though it was a decidedly unsatisfactory meeting for Joan, they finally decided to try to make it work on a "trial" basis. (That was a mistake, because Joan should have known it was a dead issue in Lucille's mind, but it was an immediate easy way out of an uncomfortable situation for both.) A few months passed, and sure enough, Joan left Fasmatic, completely frustrated and never quite knowing what had happened. If the truth were known that Lucille had never hired anyone who she thought was any smarter than she, and had never allowed a person to outshine her politically in any organization, the story might have been different. Even though Joan was well thought of at Fasmatic, it was not feasible to halt her demise. Lucille was the "new kid on the block," with all the supposed promise and potential that the new person brings to an organization, and she was not going to be second-guessed by those who had hired her. Is this farfetched? Not really. There are a dozen stories like this every day. Good performance and loyalty to the organization can all go down the drain when someone just doesn't like you. The subjectivity of human nature is a difficult thing to control, and many a good career has been subverted because of personal feelings.

We Want Our Guy in There

Another major factor in terminations is the impact of our shrinking world and the filtering-down effect of new global economy, which is causing much restructuring, downsizing and reorganization. That trend has been compounded by merger/acquisition mania, which always results in people losing jobs through redundancy or because "we want our guy in there"!

Roger was president of Power-On Company, a very successful and profitable manufacturer of heavy electrical equipment. He had done an outstanding job of keeping Power-On in the black, even though the market was being dramatically eroded by foreign competition. Power-On's parent, Formal Forest Products, was being squeezed on the bottom line, and determined that Power-On would have to be divested. Allison Manufacturing made a generous offer which was accepted. Roger was assured that with his record and his skills, both he and his key staff would be okay. It wasn't long, however, before Allison management began to restructure and consolidate, which resulted in a number of redundant staff jobs. A majority of Roger's staff got their notices, and shortly thereafter, Roger was informed he would be replaced by a member of Allison's staff.

So, even though Roger was competent and successful, as was his staff, there wasn't a need for the number of people available, and Allison's management obviously felt more comfortable with its own people in charge. It's not a question of competency, but a trickle-down economic effect.

Far-Reaching Implications

Terminations are inevitable, and have become a more common and disruptive factor in business over the last five years or so. There is a growing recognition that there are many and varied reasons "why," and although terminations are everyday occurrences, it doesn't lessen their impact on the organization or the parties directly involved.

As terminations have become more prevalent and much more publicized, it is also being recognized that terminations have implications beyond the impact on the individual being terminated. There is the impact on the firing manager, the terminated individual's family, remaining employees, stockholders, the industry, academia, and the community at large. It can be a problem of far-reaching proportions, and no longer can be dealt with as merely a Friday afternoon conversation, saying, "Your services are no longer required." You can't assume that "the words" will accomplish the deed. There are many other facts involved. It must be treated as the business problem that it is—a problem demanding all of the practicing manager's and the human resources manager's attentions and skills if it is to be the professional, sensitive and humane process it can be. Terminating should be a process that reflects well the organization as an employer and member of the community.

The Good Old Days

Terminations are truly a negative subject. It is not a subject that fits with the general business mentality or our general attitudes—it's terminal, it's the end, the finish. It is the last thing that a manager wants to have to cope with, because it is almost always a traumatic and emotional confrontation for both parties. Not too many years ago, most organizations, particularly the larger ones, would always find a place for good old Bill or Betty: "She was so loyal for all those years, we can't just put her out. We can probably find a spot for her for the next couple of years until she retires." This does not mean that terminations and layoffs because of company acquisitions and plant closings didn't happen, but they didn't seem to happen as often. There was less pressure on most businesses in the less global economy of those days. When someone had to be terminated, it was just as traumatic and emotional, and maybe even more so, because loyalty and the work ethic were key ingredients in the work force. For a number of reasons, that concept has changed as has the old concept of job security, because it is practically nonexistent today. More and more, job security today means being good at what you do so that you can always do it somewhere else. That attitude may appear selfish and self-serving, but it is practical and realistic in this highly competitive and merger-minded business world. This concept must be understood by the practicing manager and factored into personnel decisions. The economic realities of today's highly competitive global economy will only perpetuate the termination problem for years to come. This fact will ideally lead management to focus more attention on their most critical asset: people.

An employment agreement will have to reflect shared interest, shared benefits, a fair exchange on the part of both parties, and in all likelihood, some agreement on termination, because no one is "long-term" anymore.

Whether we like it or not, each year that passes indicates that fewer people have long-term careers with any one organization—nor should it be expected. It just isn't realistic to assume that everyone hired by "good old Acme Manufacturing" will spend their careers there.

Everyone Is a Potential Victim

The longer one works in this dramatically changing world of work, the greater the odds that he or she will be terminated. Everyone is vulnerable today, regardless of level, functional area, or compensation. The CEO as well as the janitor may be targeted; it isn't always just "the guys in the plant." The odds are high that, in any given career, the individual will be threatened with job loss or terminated at least once.

It would probably be impossible to determine with any accuracy the number of people terminated in the United States each year. The statistics would be difficult to compile because of the variety of terms used to designate leaving employment—*fired, laid off, early retired*—and the confusion around many terminations, particularly when at the higher levels of organizations, where more elaborate rationales tend to be developed to justify the action and to pacify the individual and the public.

The practicing manager must understand also that even though most of the talk about terminations centers around the impact on the organization, the real effect is with the individual. Terminations are very personal and usually very emotional. The manager must understand that a person's job is a critical part of his or her life, and consumes more time, thought and energy than most people realize. Just consider the time involved in commuting, worrying, thinking about, and doing your job, and it's obvious no one works just a 40-hour week. It is a substantial portion of one's life. Our jobs sustain us as individuals, and allow us to be the people we are. We are judged by what we do for a living—our occupations define us to others. So when a job is lost, whether the individual is willing to admit it or not, it is in a sense the ultimate rejection, the ego-shatterer.

Age of Litigation

Terminations have far-reaching concerns that go well beyond Quantum Manufacturing and Carl's sleepless night. The Pauls who are terminated will almost always experience anger, trauma, and emotion to varying degrees. But the biggest critics an organization has relative to terminations may well be those employees not affected. If communication isn't clear and direct so those people know what's going on and where they stand, a whole new set of problems may arise. Problems that develop with terminations almost invariably relate not to the reason *why* it was done, but rather to *how* it was handled. Most organizations have trouble expressing anything negative, and this is particularly true when it regards terminations. An ill-considered statement, or a comment made without proper forethought, often puts a company in court. There probably has never been nor will be terminations that everyone agrees with. Some employees will be waiting for the other shoe to drop and will be thinking of leaving. Furthermore, this is an age of aggressive media, and bad public relations can seriously harm any business. So if termination isn't handled professionally, it's a no-win situation.

This is also the age of litigation; everyone is a potential litigant. Arnold Deutsch, in his excellent book, *The Human Resources Revolution*, said:

> This is the age of the activist in which everyone is a litigant, not the least being an organization's own employees. People today readily take court

action against policies and practices they feel infringe upon their human rights or upon others for whom they feel a responsibility. Today's company operates within a sophisticated web of social advocacy organizations with experience in the weapons of boycotts, class-action suits, publicity, and lobbying. Uniquely, this is a revolution with substantial government support. Congress has created sweeping new kinds of social legislation. Courts have responded with financially staggering penalties on organizations found to have transgressed against these new laws, and an extensive group of regulatory agencies polices their implementation.[2]

There isn't any foolproof way to avoid the potential of a lawsuit related to terminating someone, but the wise employer will take every step to ensure that everyone involved in the recuriting, selection, placement, orientation, evaluating and termination process is oriented and kept up to date on all the nuances involved. Equal employment opportunity (EEO) laws, such as the Civil Rights Act of 1964 (Title VII in particular), and the Age Discrimination in Employment Act are the law of the land. Every personnel decision, including termination, that an organization makes is impacted by the law. Practicing managers and human resources managers must work in tandem and understand the specific requirements of the law. Otherwise, it may be up to a court to decide. The matter may then come down to the terminated employee's word against that of the organization, and who remembers, or believes, what was said on the specific date the employee was hired.

Employment at Will

According to government figures, some 60 million people in the United States are "employed at will." That statistic means that roughly 70 percent of the total work force is not covered by some form of written agreement (like a union contract) that spells out how and under what conditions they may be terminated. There are other exceptions than union contracts for the employment-at-will concept. For example, one cannot ignore the existing EEO legislation relative to age, sex, race, and so on, nor can an employer go against public policy—an individual can't be terminated for refusing to break the law, even if the boss demands it. To those restrictions, one can add the fact that in recent years there has been more willingness to write *employment contracts* for a broader spectrum of management. These may not be as detailed and comprehensive as the so-called golden parachutes that top corporate officers asked for and got not many years ago. Even the enactment of a 1984 law that imposed a stiff tax on this type of payout has not stopped organizations from giving something in exchange for talent they really need, be it middle management or top management.

For years, employers could hire and fire employees at will. They could, and would, fire without conscience and at their convenience. As reported in the *Employment Management Association Journal:*

> Courts have generally recognized an employer's right to manage its business and control its work force. Under the traditional employment-at-will doctrine, an employer legally has been able to discharge an employee-at-will at any time without notice for good cause, for no cause, or even for cause morally wrong, so long as special protective statutes and an express contract are not violated. As employee-at-will is (1) hired with no understanding that he will be employed for a definite period of time, and (2) with no limitation on the reasons for termination of employment. Consequently, employees-at-will rarely challenged their terminations in court, and those who did usually saw their lawsuits summarily dismissed. Over the last 20 years, however, many state courts have engrafted exceptions to the "at-will" doctrine. At least 43 states and the District of Columbia have recognized a cause of action for wrongful termination based on one theory or another.[3]

More and more state courts have now ruled that the right to terminate an employee may be restricted by the basic precepts of fairness, public policy consideration, statements made during the selection process by interviewers, statements in company brochures and manuals, and statements made in performance evaluations. The employment-at-will concept is being weakened, and employers, whether they like it or not, must take a hard, objective look at their personnel policies, practices and procedures. In this age of litigation, every negative decision about employees must be regarded as a potential basis for a lawsuit.

Easing Your Conscience

Another problem with terminations is the naiveté of many managers who try to ease their consciences by putting their termination rationale in one of the following perspectives.

"Everyone nowadays knows how to find a better job with better pay."

"A decent severance package will suffice and cover him through a job hunt."

"She has good credentials/experience/skills, so the phone will ring off the wall once the word gets around about her availability."

"He can always consult or start his own business."

"She will really be better off out of here, so this is really a beneficial move for her."

Woe to the manager who expresses any of those points to an employee being terminated. Losing one's job is almost always a highly emotional and negative experience, and to try to put a positive gloss on it will only compound the problem. Each of those rationales is a misconception, and each will be discussed in more detail to provide a further understanding of the depth of the problem.

What Do You Owe Employees?

The effective manager remembers that whatever the organization asks of the employee (and some of those things involve personal sacrifice, like relocation) is usually complied with because the employee assumes the organization is dependent on him or her, and vice versa. When termination occurs, interdependence ceases, and this can be a highly emotional problem for the individual and his or her family. The caring organization, however, understands that it owes some degree of support and assistance to those employees leaving "without cause."

An unwritten rule of business, and perhaps one of the most important factors in termination psychology, implies that an employment deal obligates both employer and employee. The employee is obligated to use all his or her skills and abilities to the fullest to make the employer successful. The employer is obligated to provide the direction and guidance and tools for the job. The employer also should be obligated to provide performance feedback, and if continued employment is not feasible, to provide some degree of assistance in order to ease the transition to a new job.

To make this agreement work, there must be communication. Communication is really the key to good employee relations, and thus to an effective and productive organization. Effective, productive organizations know how to communicate the good news and the bad news.

After good communication, the more specific obligations of a conscionable employer to an employee when the decision is made to terminate may cover a wide range. Obviously, what any one organization is willing and able to provide will depend on its understanding of the impact of the action in its broadest terms. Termination is an area of great sensitivity, because it is a process that is ripe for setting precedents. Precedents are fine, as long as implications are understood and are handled with discretion. The primary debts owed employees being terminated are at once specific and vague: severance pay, in some amount; honesty and realism about reasons for termination. Fully recognizing that this process seldom works the way it should because of human nature, the following are suggestions for practicing managers and human resources managers. Each obligation will be elaborated in subsequent chapters.

1. *A truthful, realistic rationale for why it's happening.* An honest explanation may be the most positive thing that can be given to the individual.

2. *Professional respect for the individual.* The absolute truth seldom comes out in these situations, but when the situation is acknowledged to be one that's not working, both parties will be better off as a result.

3. *No procrastination.* Like the ad says, "We will sell no wine before its time." The individual deserves the courtesy of termination "when it's time," and not merely when it's convenient or comfortable for the manager or organization.

4. *Some degree of financial support.* Most every organization seems to have some policy or precedent for use as a benchmark. Because severance pay is such an important and integral part of any termination arrangement, it is worth noting here the results of a recent study. The Employment Management Association 1987 surveyed 259 human resource professionals and reported a number of interesting facts concerning benefits to employees who were victims of downsizing:

90.5% provided severance (or continuation) pay

65.4% provided benefits other than those required by COBRA (Consolidated Omnibus Budget Reconciliation Act)

75.9% provided outplacement services.

Severance pay was more likely to be provided where the employee could not be held accountable for job loss. Those firms that provide severance pay do so most often when the job is eliminated in reduction in force (85.7 percent). In 63.4 percent of the companies, those who opted for early retirement as a result of a reduction also got severance pay. Fewer companies provide severance pay when the reason is one over which the employee may have some control—poor performance (24.7 percent) or dismissal for cause (5.9 percent). Severance pay is paid on a case-by-case basis by 42.1 percent of the surveyed companies.

The study indicated that other reasons for providing severance pay include: an enticement for poor performers to resign; in lieu of a notice period; and by mutual agreement to provide severance pay upon termination.

Who receives severance pay? In respondent companies who pay it, 100 percent of salaried exempt employees and 89.7 percent of salaried nonexempt employees receive it. Several responses indicated that only executives receive severance pay. Unorganized hourly workers receive it at 45.9 percent of companies, and organized hourly workers at 14.2 percent of the companies.

Determination of severance pay amount is by written policy or formula in 82.6 percent of respondent companies. Years of service is the most commonly used component of such formulas (95.9 percent). Other factors mentioned include reason for termination (45.0 percent), level of job (39.4 percent), and exempt or nonexempt status (31.2 percent). A few companies (12.4 percent) have negotiated severance pay into collective bargaining agreements.

The most common formula was one week's salary per year of service, though many respondents reported paying two weeks per year. Maximum amounts ranged from thirteen weeks to twenty-six weeks, to unlimited. Other formulas included:

One (or two) weeks salary per year of service, plus one (or two) additional weeks salary;

Severance pay accrued in accordance with vacation policy;

Four weeks salary, plus one week for each year's service, plus one additional weeks pay for each year of service over fifteen;

Employees with two or three years' service receive 50 percent of their monthly salary, and 25 percent of monthly salary for each additional year of service; and

Weeks of salary are tied to ranges of service.

Several respondents indicated they consider employee's age in determining severance pay amounts.

As to other benefits outside of COBRA requirements, 65.4 percent of respondents reported that their companies continue employee benefits for a period of time. Medical or HMO continues throughout severance in 50.7 percent of companies; for a specified period in 37.9 percent; for thirty days from termination date in 11.9 percent; and for the lifetime of an "age plus service" formula in 4.6 percent. Other benefits continuation periods included: through end of month in which employee terminates; through end of pay period; up to one year after layoff; 45–90 days; six months; and determined on a case-by-case basis. In 14.6 percent of respondents, employees are terminated from medical benefits on day of termination. Employee Assistance Programs (EAP) are not available to terminated employees of 52.2 percent of responding companies."

There are a number of good arguments for severance pay and they are not and should not be thought of as reasons to cover the sins of the organization. The overriding reason for severance pay is very logical—it is money to assist the displaced individual to make the transition to a new job without suffering any major loss financially. It should not be thought of as money paid to make someone, either the manager or the individual terminated, feel better; it is not a reward for having been around a long time; and should never be thought of as payment to soothe the emotions of an angry ex-employee.

More and more organizations, however, seem to be willing either to adjust the formula for severance pay or to consider extensions when it is apparent that a significant but unsuccessful effort is being made by the individual to find new employment. There also is great debate, particularly among outplacement practitioners, relative to the terminating of severance pay when new employment is secured. This often leads to a delay in reporting the date of new employment anyway. Experience has shown the amount of money involved to be fairly minimal, anyway, and not worth making an issue of it with all the potential side effects.

Severance pay is an important factor in how the organization is viewed by those who remain, and an important factor in the corporate culture. There is a fine line to be drawn in deciding how often and to what extent exceptions should be made. The inherent danger is that a lot of exceptions and precedents become policy-setting.[4]

5. *References.* References are an often overlooked aspect of the employment process, but are more and more critical today. There must be some type of "party line" established between the manager and the departing employee to satisfy reference needs.

6. *Job-hunting support.* Ideally, this would include the necessary logistical support, such as office and secretarial help and outplacement support, provided internally or externally by an outplacement consultant.

For terminations to be an effective management tool, it makes sense to consider them in the context espoused by J.J. Gallagher: "It's like the no-fault concept of divorce where both parties agree they are blameworthy in the break-up; that neither party is totally culpable; that both parties will suffer from the separation; and both parties will gain by living under better circumstances in the future. It is in their best interests to sever the relationship." He goes on to say that: "Not only is firing often necessary from an economic point of view, but acceptable from a social point of view. If the employment relationship isn't working, it's acceptable to terminate it, but to do it with the empathy, support and compassion necessary."[5]

The chapters that follow should allow the practicing manager and the human resources manager to develop the necessary controls and procedures to hone their skills and prepare their organizations for this most difficult and sensitive task.

2
The Termination Checklist

A Framework for the Practicing Manager

It may be more apparent now to the practicing manager that the subject of terminations and terminating is more complex and involved than previously thought. There are so many details and implications that one must consider this a very serious and complex business problem. The following chapters will provide detailed insight for the practicing manager and the human resources (HR) manager into the actual termination process by spelling out who, what, when, where, why, and how. This chapter will provide the framework for what follows by spelling out a termination checklist—factors to be considered in effecting professional, sensitive and humane terminations.

The End Justifies the Means

J.J. Gallagher has long been a proponent of orderly terminations, and I have borrowed generously from his ideas for this chapter. As he says:

> Before proceeding with any termination, ensure that all the bases have been covered—have all possible alternatives been considered? Is it truly an irrevocable situation? This should include the possibility that there may be medical/physical or emotional/psychological factors which may need to be resolved through professional assistance and may allow the individual to be salvaged.[6]

Once the final decision is made, however, this checklist approach is a necessity, because of the high degree of emotion and feeling on the part of both the manager and the individual terminated, and the always-present specter of litigation. Terminations are a particular problem because the manager wants to "get it over with." The emphasis is on the solution, instead of the process; in the desire to be done with it, the "end justifies the means."

Even though it appears that a majority of organizations have spelled out their policies and procedures relative to terminations, many still have not. The subject is constantly in the media and under discussion, but there are still people who don't get the word, and the inherent danger in that is the threat of litigation. There must be hard, verifiable facts and documents to ensure the professionalism required of terminations today.

Why a Checklist?

A termination checklist should help ensure that all the bases are covered, and that the manager will be prepared for most issues that might be raised by the employee. This checklist, when carefully conceived and realistically administered, will provide the best insurance that things will not go awry. The checklist also enables better preparation for the termination interview itself, by assisting in development of a scenario that also can be utilized for training the firing manager through a role-play dialogue. This checklist, like any of an organization's policies or procedures, will only be effective insofar as it is understood. Developing, promulgating and administering the checklist should be a primary responsibility of the human resources (HR) manager in conjunction with the practicing manager.

The HR manager must be designated as "enforcer" of the checklist. He/she should be the interpreter, with the firing manager, of how each step relates to a particular situation. The HR manager should be responsible for documenting the procedure for every termination to ensure continuity and to avoid setting unworkable precedents—a real danger in what is almost always a highly charged situation.

Assuming that up-to-date policies and procedures exist for terminations, then the organization should also be able to assume that its termination practices are legal and will meet the criteria of being humane, sensitive and ethical. With good guidelines (policies, procedures, checklist) and the proper corporate attitude, terminations can be planned and executed with the appropriate degree of precision and efficiency. The existence of a checklist will help instill the discipline necessary to make that happen.

Checklist Hot Spots

There are five basic areas to consider in developing a termination checklist. It is hoped that this checklist as presented will be all-inclusive. It should be a comprehensive document to ensure that nothing will fall through the cracks. A corporate discipline should exist for every termination so that carelessness is never an excuse. The five points are:

1. documentation—defining, verifying and recording all the necessary information about a given termination;
2. communication—what can and needs to be said internally, externally and to the individual(s) being terminated;
3. legalities—what are the obligations of the organization and the individual;
4. termination interview—the who, what, when, where, and why.

5. administrative aspects—all the loose ends relative to an employee leaving (e.g., a termination letter that specifies the organization's responsibilities and any commitments of the individual, proprietary and confidential information agreement, benefits).

Many of the details of these five points will be spelled out in policy and procedure statements, and it is incumbent upon everyone involved in a given termination to be aware and knowledgeable of all the details and implications involved. The HR manager should assume the responsibility for whatever orientation and training is necessary, and never leave the interpretation and administration of termination details to the firing manager. Utilizing the termination checklist as the basic guide in consummating the termination must be a dual responsibility of the human resources function and the firing manager.

Documentation

Terminations are done for one of three basic reasons:

1. a job is *eliminated,* whatever the rationale (acquisition or merger, cost reduction, subsequent restructuring);
2. *poor performance;* and
3. *unacceptable business behavior,* i.e. behavior outside acceptable business ethics and practice.

In practice, the real reasons for terminating are seldom discussed with the individual, because there are often very subjective environmental factors involved. As one wag puts it, "I had an illness; the boss was sick of me." Whatever the *real* reason, termination must fall into one of these three categories to be verifiable.

Factual documentation is a necessity and it should be standard practice. Policy should dictate a standard review and approval process before any individual may actually be terminated. The complexity and level of clearance necessary may be dictated by the level and or function of the individual being terminated. Often, termination of long-term employees will require final clearance from the company president, while that of other employees may only need clearance from the functional manager. The clearance procedure provides a good check and balance to the termination process, and also ensures that the required level of discipline is maintained. The HR manager should be sure that all the necessary information is compiled (in conjunction with the responsible manager), and should also review the information with the organization's counsel or law department, as circumstances dictate. If there is *any* question as to the basis for the action (the rationale), it should be automatically reviewed by counsel. No final action should be taken until each step of the documentation process has been completed satisfactorily. Critical to any documentation will be addressing any EEO or affirmative action concerns: Is the terminee over forty? A minority? Handicapped? Female? Is there any hint of sexual harassment? Any considerations like these demand strong, supporting evidence, or termination can mean trouble. If the individual is being terminated due to elimination of a job, there must be factual supporting information justifying the staff reduction and the inability to utilize the individual's skills elsewhere in the organization.

If the termination is for poor performance, there must be written appraisals confirming the facts of poor performance. A critical point will be documentation that the individual was aware of the information contained in the appraisal. Never allow information to be included in an appraisal that is not discussed and signed by both parties. This is why appraisal systems to be effective must be joint discussions and both parties must "sign off" to verify their understanding of the details discussed. There should be no exceptions or a particular situation will have no validity in the courts. Also, there *must* be a consistent approach to appraisals for everyone; if it appears that an individual is being singled out, the company is at risk. Also, the longer-term the employee, the more likely that, should there be litigation, the courts will look even harder to ensure that all the bases have been covered—has everything been done to try to help the individual? Therefore, the appraisal record becomes the key document should there be litigation regarding poor performance.

Behavior beyond the bounds of accepted business practice will also require valid and verifiable evidence that it was of the nature to discredit/ embarrass the organization. Legal experts will be invaluable here in defining the details and any precedents, should there be litigation.

Communication

Communication is the old bugaboo of organizations—and doubly difficult when it means getting people really to hear and believe negative messages. This subject, terminations, may be one of the most difficult messages of all to communicate, because of its nature. People don't want to hear it; it's a frightening subject that threatens a basic precept of their existence. It's like talking about an incurable disease—maybe if it is ignored, it will go away. Granted, it *is* an unpleasant subject, but it must be talked about with good judgment and brought out in the open for a variety of reasons, not the least of which is that so many people are affected, internally as well as externally. It may be further complicated by a level of confidentiality in certain instances that will be crucial to the solution of the problem.

Avoiding Leaks. The immediate concern about any communications usually is keeping the news from leaking until you are ready to announce it. This particularly true here because of the sensitive nature of the subject. The real problem is as so aptly put by former Admiral William "Bull" Halsey, United States Navy: "Secrets are unfortunately no longer secret when one other person knows." Leaks do occur, and this subject is one of the toughest of all to keep completely undercover—too many people are usually involved and the word somehow gets out—an overheard phone conversation, a draft memo in the wastebasket, a comment at a local bar. Should a leak occur before you are ready to go public, you have really only three choices:

ignore the situation—"no comment";

advance the termination date to immediately;

delay the action with no comment.

You really can't deny that it will happen, or you will have egg on your face when it does. The organization must use its best judgment and self-control under these conditions. A leak or a rumor may be ten times worse than the truth, but often you may have no choice but to bear with it for valid business reasons.

Need-to-Know Individuals. There will also be situations for a variety of reasons where certain individuals or other organizations will need to be informed ahead of any general release. It may be necessary, for example, to let key members of the organization know of a pending termination when it might impact their business areas or functions. There may well be situations where key customers will need to be informed as soon as possible of the pending action should the individual being terminated be crucial to a specific account. Other external contacts who may need to be clued in would include public officials who have been or are involved with projects of the organization. Also, certain government officials may have a need to know, for example, the Controller of the Currency, in the case of a senior bank official. Depending on the responsibility level of the individual to be released, it may also be necessary to inform the company's board of directors.

There are two other groups which may require some advance notice, and will most certainly require detailed input at some point. First, if the company utilizes the college campus as a recruiting resource, or is a technically oriented company with a degree of technical interchange with certain campuses, some communication to key people at those schools should be considered. The second group would include any technical societies and associations that may have members among company employees. The campus should be up to date on action taken so that they can counter any negative reactions about the organization's treatment of people. The rationale for the terminations should be specified honestly and objectively. If Professor Jones in the engineering department at State University is kept up to date, he can in turn help negate possible adverse reaction about XYZ Corp. as a good place to work.

The technical society or professional association should be the recipient of information on terminations for essentially the same reason: to negate any feelings the company is a bad place to work. No organization needs bad press from this source, which could affect future recruiting efforts.

There may be other individuals or organizations who will have a need to know to preserve relationships, but great discretion should always be exercised so that there is not a premature leak of information or a confused or garbled rationale.

Public Announcements. There are also a number of considerations here, depending on the magnitude of the problem. How much and specifically what is to be said may depend on the status of the individual in the organization. Is this a senior executive? An individual of less importance vis-à-vis impact internally and externally? Are a group of employees involved? Whatever the magnitude of the problem, there should be a plan to communicate the necessary information to meet responsibilities to all of the communities affected. This is primarily the public media, the trade press and the general employee population.

The goal should be to communicate enough information to clarify the situation, but to do it in a manner that will ideally avoid further publicity, that is provide enough information initially to satisfy the audience. The worst thing to have happen is to impair the character or ability of the group or the individual being terminated. There has been litigation based on the type of information released and the manner in which it was disseminated. The cardinal rule should be to say as little as possible and to write as little as possible—the odds go down that something will be misrepresented if the statement is concise.

Should there need to be a public announcement of an individual termination, it is wise to have both the organization's and individual's approval of what is to be said. Designate an in-touch key executive to be the spokesperson for inquires from local media sources. If the termination is of national importance where major media or trade publications might be involved, it would be best to utilize the organization's public affairs or public relations expert. Centralizing the response point alleviates the problem of communications exceeding the basic message and information agreed upon. The HR manager should play a key role in disseminating the information to the employees, and individual managers should be responsible for communicating with their employees and customers or suppliers as deemed necessary.

Data sheets (see exhibit 1) should be provided to the responsible persons in all parts of the organization for reference in responding to internal and external inquiries.

In the case of a group termination, a press release (exhibit 2) should be prepared and disseminated at the appropriate time. An announcement to affected employees should, of course, be given to each individual prior to public announcement in the media (see exhibit 3). Individual terminations should also be communicated as concisely as possible, as in the examples that follow:

External—Mr. William Touchstone, Vice-President of Manufacturing at Quagmire Chemical Corporation, has resigned to pursue other interests.

Internal—Bill Touchstone has resigned from the Corporation to pursue other interests. A replacement will be named in the near future.

Legalities

This is a difficult area, because every facet of the individual's history with the organization is interrelated to termination, and thus raises the specter of potential litigation—not only what has been said and how it was said, but what is said now and how it is said to the individual. The terms of termination, contractual obligation (real or implied), confidential and proprietary information aspects, the EEO implications can be a dangerous minefield for an organization that does not have its house in order. Amazingly, many, many organizations still terminate "by the seat of the pants"—they have no written policy or procedural guidelines, not only about terminations, but about many other aspects of personnel relations, and these are all so interrelated in current business life.

EEO Laws. In Chapter 1, it was noted that a number of laws relate to equal opportunity, and the one that has received the most attention and had the most dramatic impact is the Civil Rights Act of 1964, specifically Title VII, which essentially prohibits discrimination because of race, color, national origin, sex, or religious beliefs. This act was soon followed by other significant legislation relating to job equality and rights. Then came the Age Discrimination in Employment Act (ADEA), which prevents discrimination because of age for those persons between forty and seventy years of age. And last but not least, the Rehabilitation Act of 1973 prevents discrimination because of disability/handicap.

When considering terminations, therefore, it is important to recognize that the law provides certain protection to women, minorities, people over forty years of age, and the disabled. There must also be concern for terminations for which there is no written law on the books because of employment-at-will implications—implied contract; public policy (such as "whistle-blowing" or refusal to perform illegal acts); and unfair or malicious termination. This should be reason enough to develop a thorough plan and checklist to be followed, or the odds of litigation will rise dramatically.

The complexities of interpreting all the nuances of these statutes, plus the employment-at-will implications, may necessitate legal advice or opinion in formulating all policies, procedures, plans, or any scenario related to termination.

Employment Contracts. Employment contracts are discussed in detail in chapter 6. However, it is worth noting here that thought must be given to the possibility that things won't work out when someone is hired, and that really is the reason an employment contract is drawn up. The rationale for an employment contract is mutual protection, but often the urgency of getting that certain someone on the payroll precludes the employer from having as much protection as the potential employee. The interpretation of the contract in its finest detail should take place prior to the act of termination to ensure there is no hidden agenda for the terminated employee and to determine the organization's exact responsibilities and obligations.

Terms of the Termination. There are four basic reasons people leave an organization: *discharge,* which is management-initiated; and *layoff,* which is management-initiated; *resignation,* which is employee-initiated; *retirement,* which is also employee-initiated. Those are pretty cut-and-dried definitions, and procedurally, can be spelled out precisely. There may be situations or circumstances where it is desirable to allow the individual to choose the manner of departure. For example, an individual may opt to "resign" rather than face the public as someone who was "let go." It is good practice in that circumstance to clarify each party's obligations (see exhibit 4). The wisdom or validity of that approach can be debated; however, many organizations will offer an individual options in certain circumstances. There are basically four options available.

> *Resignation,* even though it is forced, often can be a face-saver for the individual as well as the organization.
>
> *Early retirement,* which may simply be a version of resignation, can be appropriate in many circumstances. There is no real stigma to "going early."
>
> *Transfer* to a special assignment, which even though it may be a real job, is a transparent ploy, solves nothing, and usually only prolongs the agony. In reality it confirms or denies nothing for public consumption.

Termination, which is the only other option if the other three are not considered desirable by the individual.

Before those choices are offered, the organization should give hard thought to the possible implications. They should never be used as an "easy way out." This is the strongest argument for having a specific policy statement on terminations, and another good reason for having a procedure and checklist that considers precedents and all the implications of exceptions.

Specific Precautions. A number of other items may need specific attention with each individual being terminated, and the following, at a minimum, should be part of the termination checklist:

Salary. Pay is due for work done, plus pay for accrued vacation. Failure to pay promptly could violate most labor laws.

Bonuses. Should there be a proportion of an individual's annual bonus based on the person having worked a portion of the year? It would be wise to consult your legal expert and examine precedents.

Benefits. Money due through pension and/or profit-sharing plans, for example, should be paid. Employee Retirement Income Security Act (ERISA) regulations require this.

Stock/loans. There may be stock or stock options that must be redeemed or sold back within a certain time frame. Are there loans or advances to be accounted for?

Confidentiality/proprietary information agreements. The individual being terminated must get a copy of the signed agreement. If agreements don't exist, try to reach an agreement on such things as pending patent applications. In terms of non-compete agreements, you might add the necessary words to any termination agreement (see exhibit 5). These are difficult to enforce in their finest detail, with the possible exception of trade secrets; however, such an agreement may prove to be a deterrent for the disgruntled ex-employee. Fortunately, a majority of employees will honor certain business ethics and business morality, but even so, this is a point worth discussion.

References. What information will the organization provide, by policy? Many organizations only *verify* dates of employment, salary and position held because of potential litigation by ex-employees and hiring organization. This is another difficult and sensitive aspect of terminations.

You should have a reference information release form if you feel obligated to provide detailed information (see exhibit 6).

For officers and other executives, additional points may need specific attention. Company directors elected by stockholders cannot be fired as such. They can be terminated from their jobs as company officers and not renominated for directorship when their terms expire. Check that signing authority and any other legal and financial duties be withdrawn. Bonding and liability insurance should be canceled. These actions must be consistent and in strict conformance with the organization's bylaws.

There may be other items besides those mentioned here; however, your checklist and an employee fact sheet (see exhibit 7), and involvement of the responsible people, i.e. legal and human resources staff, will help to ensure that all the bases are covered and that a professional and humane termination scenario will be developed for every situation.

Termination Interview

Chapter 3 discusses the termination interview in some detail. However, it is worth noting the key points here so that the termination checklist is all-inclusive and specifies the steps and responsibilities to be considered.

Personal Considerations. A first step in planning a termination interview, and a particularly sensitive aspect of any termination, will be a thorough check of the individual's personnel file and a review of personal knowledge for any information that might affect the basic approach to the situation. The following points are too often overlooked and may compound the severity of the termination's impact.

What is the individual's medical situation? Under treatment for any medical condition? Is there a history of heart problems? Any other known problems that may be aggravated by the termination? What is the individual's emotional state? These points are important in ascertaining the immediacy and kind of assistance the individual may require, which could involve professional help.

Significant dates, like employment anniversary, birthdays, holidays, should be avoided. The planned date should also be reviewed in terms of pension, bonus, and other benefits eligibility.

Are there family circumstances, such as family illnesses, dependent parents, recent financial obligations, etc., that indicate the need for special support systems?

Does the individual anticipate his or her termination? How much of a surprise/shock will the interview be?

The Final Interview.

Who. The responsible manager (the boss) must be the one who gives the message. There may be circumstances in which another person (preferably an HR representative) should be present, either as a witness or as support for an anxious manager. In what are assumed to be particularly stressful circumstances, it might be wise to consider having an outplacement counselor "on hand," on standby.

What. The termination message should be irrevocable. Therefore, all procedures must be complete, all clearances obtained, and so on. The "termination letter" should be prepared.

When. A termination should not be done on a Friday or the day before a holiday; that just prolongs the agony and allows resentment to build. Terminating earlier in the week allows time to provide follow-up within twenty-four hours.

Where. The best setting is private and neutral, a spot the firing manager can "escape" from, like a conference room or an empty office. It should *not* occur in a social setting, such as over lunch.

Why. This will be the crucial point and will be the basis for the terminated individual's "party line" (what will be said publicly to potential employers). Be prepared to discuss the reasons objectively, factually and rationally.

Administrative Aspects

Termination Letter. It is good practice to prepare a termination letter. It gives the individual terminated a written confirmation of the termination interview dialogue and covers all the other necessary administrative bases. There is really a twofold value in preparing this letter. First, it reinforces in writing that the termination is real and irrevocable. This should minimize or eliminate any disbelief about what's happened. Second, it provides a formal summary of what was said. Most people hear what they want, and in this upsetting situation, many details of the conversation will not be remembered if they are not put in writing.

The tone of the letter should be professional and businesslike; it should say what needs to be said and no more. There should be no personal comments (feelings or concerns), no explanations (rationale for terminating), or any superfluous information that detracts from the message of the letter. It should confirm facts and repeat pertinent details.

The items to be included in a given letter will depend on a variety of factors, such as level of the individual terminated; whether it is a no-fault layoff, or a performance-related situation; whether there are precedents. The following points can be considered as fairly comprehensive; however, because each situation is different, there could conceivably be other considerations.

Termination date—confirmation of the effective date

Severance pay/bridging pay—the dollar amount and how to be paid (lump sum or salary continuation). Is it a guaranteed amount, or is it bridging pay (pay that stops when new employment is secured)?

Vacation Pay—The dollar amount and how to be paid.

The termination letter should be signed by a responsible individual in the organization, and the terminated employee. It is also good business practice to have the document notarized for both signatories' protection.

A sample letter (exhibit 8) reflects the major items that should be covered. Obviously, each organization may have its own language and procedures; however, this sample can provide a point of departure.

Transition of Commitments. Last but not least in preparing the termination checklist is ensuring that there will be an orderly transition of all commitments. The routine of the individual to be terminated should be reviewed so that all obligations and commitments are known and will be covered, such as ongoing assignments/projects; customer obligations; convention/professional meeting attendance; speeches planned; civic, professional or business posts held as a representative of the organization. There may also be other obligations, and all of these must be considered prior to the actual termination so that appropriate parties may be informed and that there are no surprises.

The Checklist Summary

Another professional associate, Bradford Taft, president of Career Transition Group, put a good perspective on the subject of termination checklists when he spoke about planning orderly terminations before the Personnel and Industrial Relations Association of California in the fall of 1987. His talk, "Employee Discharges Gain in Complexity," urged an active stance in planning and implementing discharges. Policies and procedures must be developed so that the following areas are effectively addressed.

Definition and Verification of Reasons for Termination
Managers must be able to justify why they want to fire a subordinate, and personnel management must verify these reasons and determine if such action is warranted.

Documentation and Performance Appraisal
Effective performance appraisal systems that require proper documentation of deficiencies, adequate warnings, a definite action plan to correct the problems, and a reasonable timetable to achieve improvement must be provided to employees. When performance does not improve, then documentation exists to justify termination and to assist in avoiding a wrongful discharge lawsuit.

Communications
Management must agree on the specific reasons for firing an employee and what will be said to the individual, to the remaining work force, and to prospective employers. The content and manner in which the information is delivered are of vital importance in reducing the trauma of the termination for both the affected employee and the organization.

Separation Benefits
Severance policies should be developed that allow flexibility in determining salary and benefits continuation. It is in the best interests of the organization and the discharged employee that adequate support be provided to allow the displaced worker to find a new job as quickly as possible. A combination of salary continuation, insurance coverage, and job search assistance can speed the transition and allow for a positive ending to a negative situation.

The Termination Interview
Once it is decided to terminate an employee, and the documentation, communication and separation benefits issues have been addressed, it is time to focus on implementing the discharge. Since a determining factor as to why people file wrongful discharge lawsuits is how they are treated at the time of termination, proper planning and execution of the termination interview is of great importance.

Training the Manager
What to say, how to say it, and especially what not to say must be discussed with the manager who will do the actual firing. Attorneys are recommending that another representative, appropriately a human resources professional, sit in on the meeting to assist the manager and witness what is said. A letter outlining the major points of the conversation and listing the separation benefits should be left with the employee.

Timing
Tradition holds that employees are fired on Friday afternoon, but that is not the best time or day to deliver the bad news. Earlier in the week, and in most cases, earlier in the day are more appropriate since em-

ployees need time to recover from the shock and work out potential feelings of anger and frustration before they are ready to confront their family and friends in their personal environment. Avoiding personal significant dates, such as birthdays and wedding anniversaries, is also advisable.

Logistics
The removal of personal property should take place after or before regular working hours to reduce the potential embarrassment of both the departing and remaining employees. Arrangements for the return of company property, including keys, credit cards, and automobiles, should also be made with the dignity of the discharged employee in mind.

The location of the termination interview should also be carefully considered. Preferably, it should be in the manager's office, in private, with no interruptions.

Avoiding Wrongful Discharge Lawsuits
In today's legal climate, it is a necessity in almost all discharge situations to seek the advice of a labor attorney. In some cases, an attorney may recommend the use of a release statement, and it is important for companies to ensure that all the legal implications have been addressed.[7]

Taft concluded by stating that discharging employees is an art, not a science, and each termination situation must be treated as a unique occurrence. It must be understood that even the most thorough termination checklist must be administered with the flexibility that each individual situation requires.

Exhibit 9 suggests a format for developing a workable termination checklist. The amount of detail included may be predicated on the needs of the specific organization and its existing policies and procedures.

Exhibits

Exhibit 1: Quagmire Corporation

Quagmire Chemicals Corporation announced a 10% reduction of employees today in three locations: Bayside, Texas (75 employees); Orthington, Ohio (105 employees); and Woeful, Louisiana (32 employees).

The reason for this reduction is three-fold:

The soft economy, in particular the automobile business, a major user of our engineering plastic.

A consolidation of the Texas, Ohio, and Louisiana operating companies into a new division, Quagmire Specialties.

While sales of our VYMAR plastic have been strong, the sales of our MOTRAN plastic are well below the production capacity of the company.

All employees who are affected by this reduction will receive professional assistance in locating new employment.

Quagmire Corporation overall is experiencing a growth in sales volume due to its diversified marketplace. However, the downturn in automobile production has had significant impact on the specialties business. The long-term outlook for the Corporation is excellent, and we are committed to our goal of maintaining a significant role in the industry.

Exhibit 2: Sample Press Release

SMITH WORKERS TO LOSE JOBS

Rome, Tenn.—Most of the people employed at Smith Office Systems division learned today they are losing their jobs because of Jones Corporation plans to sell its widget business.

The Smith division on Bolt Road employs about 300 people, most of them scientists and engineers, from communities in the area, said a corporate spokesman.

About 250 employees will lose their jobs immediately, while about 50 other will remain at the plant for several months to phase out the business, the spokesman said.

He noted that the employees will continue receiving salaries for various lengths of time, and that a counseling and placement service are being set up at the facility to help them find new jobs.

The 110,000-square-foot facility occupied by Smith Office Systems was completed earlier this year and is leased by the Corporation from a partnership, the spokesman said.

The division has been developing a line of reprographic products making use of the Corporation's technology.

A statement by Daniel Posternock, the Corporation's chief executive officer, said he believes the technology has "great potential," but he added the Corporation has decided to withdraw from further development in order to focus its resources on its other products.

The action should have little or no effect on the Corporation's earnings.

Exhibit 3: Announcement to Affected Employees

(Date)

Mr. John Smith
(Present Position)

Dear Mr. Smith (John):

After a thorough and lengthy review of the economic performance of the company, management has reluctantly decided to discontinue some operations.

As a result of this decision, your position will be eliminated. Unfortunately, we have not been able to identify a new assignment for you through our internal search system.

We have engaged the services of XYZ Associates, an outplacement consulting firm, and have set up programs and procedures to help you seek new employment opportunities, and urge that you participate fully in this effort. You are scheduled to attend a Job-Hunting Workshop on (date/time).

If you choose not to attend these meetings, please contact (name), Human Resources, at 222-2222, Ext. 111.

We want to make every effort we can to help you during this difficult period to minimize any disruption in your career or personal life.

Sincerely,

Personnel Manager

Exhibit 4: Severance Agreement and Release

Boomerang Manufacturing Corporation (the Company) and Cory Henderson (Henderson) hereby agree as follows:

The Company accepts Henderson's resignation from employment as of January 19, 1988.

The Company will provide reference information as delineated in the "Henderson party line" (copy attached).

The company shall pay Henderson severance pay equal to one year's compensation, (total gross amount) $75,000. This will be paid in equal semi-monthly payments (less required deductions), with first payment on January 29, 1988, and final payment on January 15, 1989.

The execution of this agreement shall not be construed as an admission of a violation of any statute or law or a breach of any duty or obligation by either party to this agreement.

This agreement shall not be made public by either party to it.

In consideration of the foregoing, Henderson hereby releases and forever discharges the Company, its officers, employees, agents, successors and assigns, from any and all manner of actions, causes of actions, debts, claims and demands both in law and in equity, including any and all claims based upon or in any way related to employment or termination of employees, agents, successors or assigns, Henderson, his heirs, executors, administrators or assigns, ever had, now have or in the future may have for or by reason or means of any matter or thing from the beginning of the world through and until the day of the date of this agreement.

This agreement contains the entire agreement between the parties and may be changed only in writing, signed by both parties.

This release shall not be construed as a limitation upon Henderson's right to receive retirement and other benefits to which he may be otherwise entitled.

The undersigned have read and fully understand this employment severance agreement and release.

IN WITNESS WHEREOF, we have hereunto set our hands and seals this 19th day of January, 1988.

BOOMERANG MANUFACTURING CORPORATION

By _____   _____
   John Marcus   Cory Henderson
   Executive Vice-President

Exhibit 5:   Proprietary Information and Patent Agreement Letter

(Date)

Dear

This is to remind you of the legal obligations regarding proprietary rights and information of Bear Manufacturing Inc. (the Company), which you assumed when you joined the Company. As you may be aware, these obligations survive the termination of your employment with the Company and may therefore have a bearing on your future activities.

For your convenience, a copy of the applicable agreement, signed by you at the time of your employment, is enclosed.

As you will note, one of the pertinent sections concerns your obligation not to disclose information relating to the Company's business. This information relates to the Company's research, development, manufacturing, purchasing, financial, accounting, engineering, marketing, merchandising, and selling activities, where such information is proprietary, or where such information has not been made public by the Company.

This same section of the agreement further defines the Company's property rights in all papers, tools and apparatus furnished to you, or prepared by you, during your employment and your obligation to return these upon the termination of your employment.

Another section concerns the obligation for a prompt disclosure for assignment to the Company of inventions made by you individually or jointly with others while employed by the Company and during the first six (6) months thereafter.

It must be emphasized here again that these obligations survive the termination of your employment. Should you have any questions about the interpretation of this agreement, particularly as it relates to your activities after you leave, please feel free to contact the (Law Office) in (city, state) for further explanation.

Thank you for your cooperation in this matter. May I take this opportunity to wish you success in your future endeavors.

Sincerely,

Mary Hart
Manager, Human Resources

Exhibit 6:   Reference Information Release Form

PRENTICE CORPORATION

Our policy on providing reference information states that we will only *verify:*

Employment Dates
Job Title
Location
Salary

If you wish us to honor a request for reference information, i.e. employment and compensation history with Prentice Corp.; performance information; rehire status; from (name), indicate your acceptance for said information release by completing the rest of this form.

I, (name), in consideration of Prentice Corp.'s agreement to release said information, and intending to be legally bound, hereby release Prentice Corp. from any and all claims by me or through me, either known or unknown, which may arise from providing the information covered by this authorization.

_____   _____
Date   Signature

_____
Signature for Prentice Corp.

Exhibit 7:   Employee Fact Sheet

Employees will not be asked to work during their severance period/while receiving salary continuation.

Salaried employees will begin their salary continuance (amount will be the full salary in effect prior to start of salary continuance) on October 12, 1988, and will continue to be paid until new employment is secured or until the allotted salary continuance period is complete, whichever occurs first.

Should an employee apply for and receive state unemployment benefits during their salary continuance period, an amount equal to payments received will be deducted from the salary continuance.

Employees will be paid for any unused 1988 vacation entitlement with their first salary continuance check (includes any deferred vacation). Vacation may not be utilized to extend salary continuance. There will be no additional vacation entitlement should salary continuance extend into the following year.

Termination date for all employees affected will be the date salary continuance terminates or new employment begins. Employment for this purpose is defined as full-time or part-time (includes consulting, own business, etc.; anything that precludes a *full-time* job search).

Opportunities for rehire are minimal in the foreseeable future; however, the Human Resources Department will continue through the Internal Search System (ISS) to identify opportunities.

Outplacement counseling has been arranged with Carroll Associates, a highly respected outplacement consulting firm. This counseling will be in a seminar format, with additional individual follow-up counseling available. Employees are strongly urged to take advantage of this service which will prove invaluable to a job search.

Benefits (Life, Dental, Medical, and Employee Assistance Program) will continue through the salary continuance period. Long-term disability and travel accident insurance will cease on the final day of employment and commencement of salary continuance.

Details on the Profit Sharing Plan distribution and Retirement Income plan are provided in the Employee Benefits booklet. Because there are several options involved with these plans, each individual should discuss his or her particular situation with the Human Resources Department.

We want to be of every assistance to you during this period and we urge you to take advantage of the services and counsel offered.

Exhibit 8:   Termination Letter

November 12, 1988

Mr. Frederick Acres
18 Forest Road
Tampa, Florida 07203

Dear Fred:

This letter is to acknowledge your termination as Director of Manufacturing of Freda Products Corporation, which is effective as of November 13, 1988. As we discussed on November 12, 1988, your responsibilities at Freda have provided access to a substantial amount of confidential and proprietary information and knowledge of our businesses and plans, which if disclosed in any manner to others, might cause irreparable harm to Freda Products.

In light of our discussion concerning these points, we mutually understand and agree to the following:

1. Contingent upon your continued and professional performance of the obligations described in this letter, we agree to compensate you at the rate of $4,000 biweekly during the period beginning November 13, 1988, and terminating December 1, 1989. In the event of your death before all of these payments have been made, any amounts will be paid to your estate.

2. During this period while we are making separation payments as described in no. 1, it is agreed that you will not accept employment with any competitor of Freda Products without prior written consent from us. It is also agreed that these separation payments are in lieu of and not in addition to any unemployment compensation benefits for the same months or any payments for the same months we might be obliged to make as called for under the non-compete provisions of your Patent and Secrecy agreement dated March 8, 1979. Should you receive any such payment for the same months, we will deduct a comparable amount from the payments described in no. 1 of this letter.

3. Your Patent and Secrecy Agreement, signed March 8, 1979, is hereby ratified and confirmed. A copy of the agreement is attached for your information.

4. As discussed, you will turn over all the records and property in your custody or possession that belong to or relate in any manner to the affairs of Freda Manufacturing Corp.

5. Your company automobile will be available for your continued use during the period stipulated in no. 1. Should you accept new employment during that period, its availability will cease.

6. Your group accident and long-term disability insurance terminates on the effective date of your termination. Unless you decide otherwise, group life insurance will continue through the period of separation payments or until the end of the month following the month in which you take other employment, whichever occurs first. Your regular deduction will continue for group medical insurance. Your group life coverage will require you to pay the premium, including the first one-times-salary amount previously paid by the company.

7. You may be eligible to extend your medical and dental benefits beyond the severance agreement period under the provisions of the Health Care

Benefit Continuation Policy. The Director of Compensation and Benefits will provide further information on this.

8. Under the company retirement plan, your rights have vested and it will be your responsibility to notify us of your election with respect to benefits under the plan. Further details of the plan are included in your Retirement Plan booklet.

9. The distribution of your Savings Plan Account balance shall be paid within sixty days from the end of the month in which your withdrawal form is received. Payment will be made per your instructions, that is, lump sum or in equal annual installments. Further information on the plan is included in your Savings Plan Account booklet.

10. Any vacation pay accrued through November 18, 1988, will be paid to you with your first biweekly separation payment check.

11. Any personal advances due the company for the Credit Union will be deducted from the cash amounts otherwise due to you hereunder.

12. You are entitled to have the balance of your account in the Employee Stock Ownership Plan (ESOP) distributed in cash shares of Freda Manufacturing common stock (plus cash for fractional shares). Contact the Director of Compensation and Benefits for further information and to indicate your preference.

13. All cash payments to be made to you under this agreement are subject to withholding for federal income tax, and where applicable, to withholding for social security or unemployment compensation taxes.

14. You agree to notify us in writing prior to the start date of your new employment.

This letter represents the entire agreement between us and can only be modified in writing. If the foregoing conforms to your understanding of our agreement, please sign the enclosed copy and return it to me via registered mail. Upon receipt, this agreement shall become a binding agreement between you and Freda Manufacturing Corporation, 322 Palm Blvd., Tampa, Florida 07202.

Very truly yours,

FREDA MANUFACTURING CORP.

By:
Title:

(As noted before, for both parties' mutual protection it is prudent to have the termination letter notarized to avoid any confusion or discussion at a later date. A statement such as follows should be sufficient.)

(Employee's name) acknowledges that he/she has read and understood this agreement and releases and further acknowledges that he/she has had the opportunity to review it with an attorney. *(Employee's name)* further acknowledges that he/she is executing this agreement and release voluntarily and with full knowledge of its terms and provisions and of his/her legal rights with regard thereto.

(Signature of Employee)

DATE: _____

State of _____

County of _____

On _____, 1988, before me personally came *(Employee's name)* sworn by me to be the individual who executed the foregoing release and he/she duly acknowledges that he/she executed same.

_____
Notary Public

Exhibit 9: Termination Checklist

Name _____   Responsible Manager _____

Title _____   Human Resources
                                        Coordinator _____

Location _____

1. Documentation   *Comments*

   _____ Job eliminated   _____

   _____ Performance   _____

   _____ Unacceptable behavior   _____

   _____ Clearances   _____

   _____ File complete   _____

   _____   _____

2. Communication

   _____ Responsible spokesperson   _____

   _____ Need-to-Know individuals   _____

   _____ Public announcements   _____

_____ Internal announcements   _____

_____   _____

_____   _____

3. Legalities

_____ EEO implications   _____

_____ Employment contracts   _____

_____ Terms of termination   _____

_____ Specific precautions (salary,   _____
bonuses, stock options,   _____
confidentiality agreement, official   _____
duties, etc.)   _____

_____   _____

_____   _____

4. Termination interview

_____ Who   _____

_____ What   _____

_____ When   _____

_____ Where   _____

_____ Why   _____

_____ Personal considerations   _____

_____ Role play   _____

_____   _____

5. Administrative aspects

_____ Outplacement service   _____

_____ Payroll notified   _____

_____ Termination letter   _____

_____ Legal approval   _____

_____   _____

Date completed _____ Responsible Manager _____
                                                   (Signature)

3
The Termination Interview

A Manager's Most Difficult Task

Conceivably the most difficult task that any manager faces is conducting a termination interview. Faced with the responsibility of saying the words *your services are no longer required,* the strongest person can get "the shakes," sleepless nights, and sweaty palms. The termination interview, like so many other aspects of being a manager, is a skill that needs to be developed. Effective managers must be able to make and carry out termination decisions for the good of the organization. If they can't, they may be the next victims through their own procrastination.

The termination interview is the ultimate criticism, and in most instances, criticism is not easy either to give or receive. Termination interviews are a confrontation for both terminator and terminated. Initially, the terminator experiences the concern, stress and trauma until the announcement is made. Then it's the employee's turn to react. This is a process that ranges the complete emotional spectrum, and if it is to be handled well, it will require all one's interpersonal and interviewing skills. However, this is a different type of interview; different sensitivities and different skills are needed.

A Different Kind of Interview

An interview is defined as a "formal meeting in which a person or persons question, consult or evaluate another or others." That means a mutual exchange of data for evaluation purposes. In the strictest sense, then, a well-conducted termination interview may not be an interview per se, but rather a formal communication session, a conversation for one individual to pass along a message to another individual. In its simplest definition, this is a conversation to inform an employee that he or she no longer has a job with the organization. It's not a debate; it's not a time for reminiscing; it's not a time for venting anger. It is the time to convey an irrevocable message with the proper amount of empathy and understanding. In the termination interview, all the critical data that the firing manager needs to know should be available and assimilated before meeting with the person to be terminated, so it is not a data development process (as in a selection interview, for example). This is a critical distinction, because if this is conducted as an "interview," it may become a debate and a rehash of the past—exactly what it should not be.

What a Manager Really Needs to Do

An important point needs to be made here. The manager responsible for terminating must gain at least a basic understanding of the psychology of this process, an understanding of not only his or her own feelings and reactions, but also of the feelings and impact on everyone else affected, such as family, other employees, even stockholders. Chapter 4, A Manager's Perspective, is "must reading." While most managers are capable of hiring qualified people, many lack the skills required to conduct the termination process effectively. With the employment-at-will concept challenged in the courts with increasing frequency, managers must develop this skill in order to protect the employer from potential litigation and, at the same time, preserve the rights and self-respect of the affected employee.

Even though it is not an interview per se, the termination interview needs the same thought and attention to detail that a good selection interview does. Any interview, to be truly effective, must be planned with specific objectives in mind. There must be the necessary time to ensure that all the details are covered. Above all, the responsible manager must never assume expertise with termination interviews just because he has had experience hiring people. Each interview, regardless of the reason for it, is different, because every person is different and unique. The worst mistake any interviewer can make is to become too mechanistic and structured. Everyone reacts differently to being told "you're through," and everyone will reflect some degree of anger, and that must be watched to ensure that the objective does not get lost in the heat of battle.

The methodology of the termination interview is not difficult to grasp; implementing the methodology is the real problem. All interviewers, to be effective, must thus recognize their shortcomings, weaknesses, and prejudices. Self-knowledge permits greater objectivity and honesty, which are the key to the effectiveness of any interview. Interviewing for whatever reason cannot be dismissed as just another burdensome personnel task. This conversation impacts on the two key parties to it, and possibly on the whole organization, depending on the particular circumstances. In the termination interview the terminator must listen. A bad listener is almost always impatient, and there is no room for that because it may complicate the situation.

Protected Classes Terminations

The termination of females, minorities and other protected classes may demand increased objectivity and understanding of one's own biases, as well as those of the person being terminated. Bear in mind the following thoughts:

Women and members of minority groups may expect unfair treatment because of past experiences.

They may believe the only positive action relative to them results from pressure by government and top management.

They may be more perceptive about you, the firing manager, and the organization than other employees.

They may feel they had to be better prepared to do their jobs than other employees, and may want to get very specific about their shortcomings as perceived by you.

They may have an above-average understanding of employee rights and the law.

To counter the impact of those points, consider the following as you plan the interview.

Set the stage for the termination message by explaining the rationale and procedure.

Do not try to explain or justify the EEO posture of the organization.

Concentrate on the facts of the situation and avoid as much as possible the personal aspects.

Do not be ingratiating or try to deceive anyone.

Avoid any stereotypic references that relate to any one group.

The termination interview is a more volatile, more uncomfortable situation than possibly any other type of interview; therefore, it is critical that the bases of good interviewing are understood. Like all interviews, this interview is plagued by a variety of human nature problems: we talk too much, we jump to conclusions, we allow our prejudices to get in the way, we communicate to people how we want them to respond, and we often fail to translate/digest the facts we hear for appropriate action. The inability or unwillingness to listen is critical, because neither party will receive the data needed. We don't *listen*, because we would rather *talk*. Very importantly, prejudice is the enemy of good listening and so has no place in any interview. Prejudice is particularly dangerous in the termination scenario because of the emotional level that already exists.

Because the termination interview's primary purpose is to inform the person that employment is ended, it should strive to accomplish that purpose with the least possible emotion, anxiety and bad feelings. In most instances, a reasonable person will not argue much about honest, objective straightforward statements. However, all information (i.e. job-related issues only) must be discussed in an impersonal manner. This interview is a true test of the organization's employee relations posture, as well as its public relations image.

The Defensive Employee

Once the words are said by the firing manager, the terminated employee may begin playing a difficult role, which probably will be defensive, for obvious reasons. Many individuals realize that they have some bargaining power, because there are almost always some guilt feelings on the organization's part about letting someone go, as well as some guilt on the part of the firing manager. The employee in most instances will be unprepared emotionally, logistically and financially, and won't understand or agree with the decision made. Sensitive communication is needed to ensure that the necessary information relative to each of these problems is transmitted and understood. The employee may very well have a number of thoughts, not the least of which may be:

1. The individual may try to take advantage of what is clearly a difficult situation for the firing manager.

2. He or she may use threats or innuendo, for example "You know I'm forty-five years old"; "I watch you when Betty is around and I think you picked me to go because you like her looks"; "You know how much *I know* about manufacturing widgets."

3. He or she may argue that the performance appraisal system is unfair and biased, and that performance really means nothing in this decision.

4. He or she may challenge everything said in an attempt to bait the manager into some statement that may compromise him or the organization: "Would you repeat that?" "I don't think I understand that." "Why?"

5. He or she will demand an explanation of the firing manager naïve enough to say things such as "You really are too good for this job anyway"; "I know just how you feel"; "You'll probably find an even better job."

6. He or she will reject meaningless generalizations. This interview is the time for facts and precise action.

William Morin, chief executive officer of Drake Beam Morin, outplacement consultants, notes four types of responses the manager can expect to the termination message, and some approaches to defuse hostility.

Usual Response

expressions of hurt, anger, resentment, disagreement.

verbal attack on the company and its policies, possibly on the terminator.

the above reactions change to practical concerns, like "How long will I have to look?" or "Will I have access to secretarial services?"

This is the *usual* reaction of persons to terminations.

Controlled Response

Anger, hurt, resentment are held in.

Can be misinterpreted as a good response. (In a very few cases, the response actually *is* relief and the termination seen as an opportunity.)

Individual *may* not have accepted the reality of having been fired, or thinks that somehow something will save him.

May "blow up" later, at the local bar or with colleagues back in the work areas.

Might try to get revenge on the company or the terminator at a later time.

Terminator must make sure that the other person clearly understands what has happened and has the opportunity to come out of his/her shell. If necessary, the manager must use questions like "How do you feel about all this?" to draw the person out.

Hostile Response

Overreacts, openly and loudly critical of company and/or terminator.

Terminator must remain calm and not react defensively.

Once the individual calms down and starts asking practical questions, he or she usually reacts rationally and will cause no further trouble.

Only if there is a danger of physical violence or totally unacceptable behavior should individual be restrained and told that this will not be tolerated.

Shocked Response

Is very similar to the controlled response.

In the extreme, can be very quiet or cry uncontrollably.

This response is most typical of persons who later attempt suicide or have an accident.

Take time to get individual to discuss feelings. Get the person to react by asking questions about concerns, home life, immediate plans.

If there are strong symptoms of shock, the person needs immediate counseling with a professional. Refer them directly to a responsible person.[8]

It is obvious from reading those definitions that there can be situations well beyond the capability of the manager charged with doing the termination. This is all the more reason to have a plan (the checklist) for each termination that covers all contingencies, including referral points for those situations that are unmanageable.

Death, Divorce, and Termination

The major problem with any termination is that it is a task that no one really likes to perform. Because it is an odious task and one to be dreaded, the person charged with the task wants to get it over with quickly; as a result, it gets little thought or planning. The result is that too often the firing manager and the terminated employee go away not knowing what really happened, because both were anxious and upset, and didn't listen because they were unprepared. Once the words are spoken, the terminated individual will probably hear nothing else. The roles of both parties must be understood because of the usual severity of the reaction. The shock, trauma, and ego damage of being terminated has been likened to death of a loved one or divorce. In many instances, unfortunately, there is little or no sympathy connected with losing a job, as opposed to the degree of sympathy with death or divorce. Part of the rationale for this lack of sympathy, as mentioned earlier, is that people are judged by what they do for a living, and when that is disrupted there is usually a negative reaction. The unspoken attitude is: "What's wrong with you? You must be incompetent . . . what did you do wrong?"

Intellectual and Emotional Reactions

There aren't many sure things in life, but there is one sure thing in the termination process: the reaction of anger, fear, self-pity, and shock. For the responsible manager to make this an effective process, then, this reaction must be understood. Also, as Laurence Stybel of Babson College states, there is an "intellectual" and an "emotional" recognition of being fired. The intellectual side says, "Okay, it's happened, but I'm a mature person and recognize that business is business; these things happen." The emotional side says, "I'm mad as hell and I want to do something about it." This recognition may be delayed for varying periods of time. It may happen when the person is told, or it may be a day, a week, or a month later. Both of these feelings exist, and their intensity will depend on how the termination process is conducted in its entirety.

Who, What, When, Where, and Why?

Each of these points, *who, what, when, where* and *why,* is a crucial aspect of an effective termination interview, and each must be thoroughly understood.

The question of *who* is simple and logical. The responsibility for terminating rests with the manager (supervisor/boss) of the individual who is to be released. The only credible person to convey this difficult message is the manager. If the manager is not willing to assume that responsibility, then he or she is *not* performing at management level.

Betty Carlisle, human resources manager at Flexible Manufacturing, was stopped in the cafeteria one day by the vice-president of marketing, Frank White. He told Betty that he was going to be out of town on a new proposal for a week or so, and needed a favor. The favor, he explained, was that he needed to terminate Jane Green, one of the more senior people in his department; could Betty handle it while he was away? Betty knew that the relationship between Frank and Jane had been deteriorating for some time and that it was extremely sensitive. It was also obvious to Betty that as tough-minded as she knew Frank to be, he just never had been able to face up to this type of confrontation. He justified his approach to Betty saying that because it was a personnel problem, it should be handled by the personnel department. Frank also said, "Because you are both women, it would be easier for you to tell her." Betty, knowing the details of the situation and the documentation that existed concerning Jane's performance over the last year or so, politely explained the procedure to Frank—that it was his responsibility as Jane's manager, regardless of how distasteful a task it might be. She arranged a meeting with Frank that afternoon to develop a detailed checklist for Jane's termination, and even set up a role play of the termination interview to assist Frank in performing this difficult task.

The *what* of the termination interview is also very basic and very logical: to get the message across that "your services are no longer required" and that it is an irrevocable decision. The message must be delivered in a clear, concise, and efficient manner, leaving no room for misunderstanding.

Bill Evans knew he must release Jim Manning today. Bill was suffering all the usual symptoms of pre-termination and hadn't even been able to keep his breakfast down. He sat down with Jim in the late morning and told him: "I've got to let you go, Jim. I think very highly of you and we have always gotten along, but Ralph (Vice-President, Manufacturing) has never liked you and you have to go." A classic situation; Bill taking the easy way out by blaming Ralph—or so he thought. Actually, all Bill did was compound the problem and cause a very emotional confrontation between Ralph and Jim. So, it is essential to have all the facts, know what is to be said, and be sure that it is delivered in a factual and direct manner and with finality.

When to terminate is also very crucial and may be instrumental in the success of the scenario. As indicated in chapter 2, the personal aspects should be considered, such as birthdays, anniversaries, family illnesses. Experience indicates that Friday is the worst day of the week for terminations, because the weekend offers two days for the individual terminated to stew and fret and get mad (or madder). Weekends seem to allow time for thoughts of lawsuits to develop.

Cliff had made the decision to terminate Bert Jones, his manager of quality control. He had done a reasonably decent job of planning the actual dialogue of the interview. However, he had procrastinated about when to do it, and finally on Friday at 4:00 P.M. he called Bert to his office and delivered the message. Bert exhibited the usual amount of shock and re-minded Cliff that this was the weekend his only son was graduating from college and they had a big party planned—that as a matter of fact, Cliff and his wife had been invited!

All the details must be considered before the actual message is delivered. In this instance, waiting until the following week would have been better. The timing of the termination is too often predicated on the manager's desire to get it over with and have a nice weekend, regardless of the impact on the individual and his or her family's feelings and reactions. Monday through Thursday are much better days. The employee can be told early in the day, and then allowed to exit the premises with as little loss of face as possible, with the next step arranged (e.g., "Come in at 9:00 A.M. tomorrow and we will get all the severance arrangements spelled out in detail").

Where to conduct the termination interview can greatly influence its effectiveness. Again, experience suggests that the best place should be a neu-tral territory, not the manager's or employee's office. The firing manager should arrange a neutral location so each party is more easily able to leave after the interview.

Tom was very nervous about having to release Sam, one of his salesmen, but things just hadn't been working for several months. There had been a number of discussions about Sam's lack of results and reasons, but nothing had improved. Morale in the sales department was suffering because of Sam's lackluster performance.

Tom had known Sam for a number of years and thought, I'll take him to lunch; a pleasant environment will make the bad news easier to take. Tom picked up Sam at noon and they went to a nice restaurant nearby. After ordering and downing a drink, Tom began his termination speech, meanwhile ordering another round. Sam, as could be expected, took strong exception with the message. He immediately launched into a rebuttal pitch: "Tom, you have known me all these years! You can't just fire me; you know I will have a tough time finding something else."

Tom repeated that the decision was irrevocable, which only made Sam more upset, turning up his voice volume until everyone in the restaurant could hear. "Damnit, Tom, this will devastate my wife and family, and who is going to hire me now that I'm fifty? How about some compromise? I have to make a living—doesn't the company care?"

Taking the easy way out of a ticklish situation that was fueled by alcohol and the environment, Tom promised to go back and try to work something out. This interview is a perfect example of what can happen when terminations aren't handled in a professional and businesslike atmosphere.

The *why* of the termination is the key, and is critical because it is the *real message*. Keeping a person in a job should require, from any organization's viewpoint, that the person be competent and productive. If not, the whole organization, regardless of size, may suffer; or, depending on the scope of responsibility of the person, it may endanger the organization. One incompetent employee can affect many others. An organization's business code should be formulated on performance standards, and when those standards are not met, action should be taken to correct it. This may mean termination of the individual from the organization.

Realistically, however, the *why* often relates to factors more subjective than competence in one's functional area. As a result, few organizations really ever tell the whole truth to a terminated employee, because it is a very difficult and sensitive task. Often if the "real" reason *is* revealed, the implications may be horrendous.

One seldom knows, therefore, the specific reasons for being terminated. The manager and the organization will usually gloss over the real reasons by using some rationale that relates the termination to conditions beyond their control. In this writer's years of experience, I can't remember ever hearing, "I don't like you, so you're fired," or, "You are incapable of performing this job because you don't know enough." Accepting the fact that the truth seldom outs, then, the manager can work towards developing the most acceptable rationale to the organization and employee.

This *why* becomes the basis for "the party line"—what is to be communicated to the public, to the organization, and to the job market by the individual. The party line really consists of two phases. First is the actual words said in the termination interview itself, which should be brief. After the formal termination interview is over and cooler heads prevail, the second phase should happen. The individual will want to know what the organization will say when asked for references in the interview process with a potential new employer. The best approach seems to be to ask the individual to write out what he or she would want said about the situation, and then to clear it with the firing manager. In most instances, this eases the sensitivity of the situation for both parties and results in an acceptable rationale.

Ralph Adams, executive vice-president (EVP) of Operations, a relatively new hire in a newly established position at Framms Manufacturing Company, had never lived up to the expectations since he was hired eighteen months before. Framms was having problems before Ralph arrived, and things had gotten worse for a variety of reasons. Some problems were attributable to consolidation of some operations, some to declining sales and lack of new products. Ralph's problem, however, was rather basic: he should have never been hired. It was a bad decision, as he never fit the Framms culture. He was an egocentric, tough, demanding, and rather insensitive manager. Ralph, too, had felt he was in the wrong environment after he had been at Framms for about ten months.

Don Wales, the president, finally terminated Ralph. He essentially told Ralph that the chemistry was all wrong in putting him in the operations job, and in both Framm's and Ralph's best interest, the best solution was for Ralph to seek a new opportunity. Framms was going to provide generous severance and outplacement assistance and be fully supportive. This is a direct and honest reason why, but "bad chemistry" often connotes a lot of negative things and should be soft-pedaled. The second phase of the why—the external party line—was worked out to Ralph's and Don's satisfaction as follows: "Ralph was recruited away from Millington Manufacturing Corporation for a newly established position of EVP Operations. It has become apparent that the recent consolidation of activities and subsequent restructuring have eliminated the need for an Operations job at his level. There is not another opportunity available in Framms and I have discussed the situation with Ralph. He agreed that his career goals and objectives cannot be met here. On an amicable basis and with our full support, he will be seeking a new position." The statement covers all the bases and does not reflect negatively on Framms or Ralph; it just says it's a mismatch of desires, in a sense.

The party line is a funny piece of the puzzle inasmuch as someone seeking a new job must be able to explain why he or she is available, even though the answer is usually received with a certain skepticism by a potential employer, who assumes something went wrong. In the final analysis, however, they probably won't care why, as long as it is determined that the individual didn't do something unacceptable by good business standards.

Irrevocable, Professional, Not a Debate

Once the decision has been made that termination is necessary and the checklist has been completed, it should be an unalterable fact. The terminating manager should be prepared, and most importantly, understand what a severe emotional shock termination can be when people experience this degree of disruption in their lives. They will hear what they want to hear, and in these circumstances, after they hear that they are being terminated, they may react with anger, fear, self-pity, shock, threats, etc.

To be truly effective and professional, the termination interview must be at a minimum:

impersonal (the discussion is on job-related issues only);

completely accurate as to facts, so there is no confusion in terminee's mind about what has taken place;

professional, brief and concise, calm and unemotional, humane and sensitive.

To accomplish this difficult task, the firing manager should also remember that:

discussion of past events only prolongs the agony and stirs more emotion;

the firing manager must control the interview and direct thinking to the future;

preparation will go a long way to negate emotional over-reaction;

the firing manager cannot react at the level of the terminated individual, who may become hysterical, use threats or vulgarities, and may attempt to bait them;

nothing can be assumed, and the firing manager should always expect the unexpected.

Above all, losing one's job is about as negative a thing as a person can face, and the last thing he or she needs to hear are generalizations that many naïve managers espouse. These classical misconceptions only underscore the need for the manager to understand the ramifications of terminations and particularly of what they say, and to prepare thoroughly for terminations. These generalizations usually go as follows.

Everyone knows how to find a better job. Very few people know how to find a new position, especially the "right one," in a reasonable time frame.

Most people who are terminated are in the position of *being forced to look* probably for the first time since they left college. Even those people who may have made several job changes may not be very adept at job hunting. Many job changes come about because a company recruits a desired individual away from his or her current employment. When a person is terminated, he or she has to get out and *make* it happen. Finding a new position efficiently is difficult when one is coping with all the emotion and self-doubt that is experienced. People learn by doing (experience) and job hunting is not a task experienced often enough to ensure its efficient accomplishment. Job hunting is a business problem, and requires the same degree of logic, commonsense, and hard work to solve as any business problem does. Unfortunately, few people ever put job hunting in this context.

Decent severance will see them through. Few severance packages cover all the contingencies. (At the very senior levels, there are obviously situations where the financial arrangements may be quite lucrative and provide the basis for financial security.) How much severance is enough? There probably isn't a concise answer, but ideally the time frame to make a transition is considered when determining the amount. The amount of the severance package may or may not be sufficient if judged by the standard rule-of-thumb of job hunting—a month of looking for each $10,000 of salary. Experience has shown that at the more senior levels of compensation ($100,000 +), it is not unusual for it to take at least a year to find a comparable position. There is no magical formula because of the variables. To minimize the financial loss to the individual, an action plan designed to find another appropriate job must be created and implemented quickly, professionally and effectively, and that is where outplacement assistance may play a key role.

Good credentials will start the phone ringing. This may be the biggest fallacy about terminations. Often the terminating organization assumes that because it "always hires good people," the individuals can easily find a new position. Certainly an individual with good credentials, someone known in his or her field, can cope with termination better by developing more leads; however, there is more to it than that. The person who assumes that his or her known availability will start the phone ringing is probably in for a rude shock. Too many displaced people immediately bang out a resumé, buy a roll of stamps, prepare an inadequate cover letter, send the package off to a list of employment agencies or executive search firms, and then sit back and wait for the phone to ring. Or they answer all the ads in the local paper and the *Wall Street Journal,* and wait for the phone to ring. Successful job hunters must *make* the phone ring by utilizing all the resources and techniques available and not waiting for someone else to make it happen.

There's always consulting or your own business to fall back on. A great idea, given the proper thought, which means more realistic and logical thought than most people are willing to give when they have been terminated. The bottom line on both of these is that there is no such thing as a free lunch: what is one willing to sacrifice to be successful at either of these vocations? The odds are that both require harder work, more hours and less guaranteed, *regular* paychecks than a job in industry. That doesn't mean that more money can't be made, but it may not be the same amount each week, and it also means looking out for one's own benefit package. It may mean adjusting to a whole new lifestyle. Being on your own means changing your work habits. Most people who have worked for an organization don't really want the inconvenience and uncertainty posed by either of these alternatives. As a generalization, it is the exceptional person, in terms of self-confidence, who will make a success of either of these endeavors.

They will be better off, so this is really beneficial to them. Granted, in the final analysis, the individual *may* be better off by finding a good, or better, different job. However, there is a period of time during the dislocation process when no one is better off. There is the emotional strain, the financial strain or concern, strain on the family; so don't assume or tell people they are better off at this point in time. This is a negative situation and a disruption to life that is never pleasant and never forgotten.

With these points in mind, the firing manager then should follow the five rules for the termination interview, which are:

1. *Present the situation in a clear, concise and final manner.* Don't confuse the message to be delivered. Don't drag it out. "Betty, you no doubt are aware that the organization has eliminated some jobs. I must tell you that one of them is yours." Remember, only a few minutes, and no bargaining or compromise. It's irrevocable. No excuses (such as Bill Evans placing the blame on his superior!).

2. *Avoid debates or a rehash of the past.* Arguments about past performance only compound bad feelings that may exist. Do not shift responsibility; the person is your responsibility, so accept that as a fact. Say what needs to be said and shut up!

3. *To make the termination interview most effective* and to remove as much of the emotion and trauma as possible, don't ever talk down to the individual. Make the point that it's a situation that isn't working and that the decision is made. Be tactful. Don't make excuses or apologies; it's a business decision. Say something positive, for example, "we are going to help with your transition." Avoid discriminatory remarks, such as "At your age, I'd be thinking of early retirement"; or "You really

haven't kept up with the young research people who just finished their Ph.D.s."

4. *Empathetic, but not compromising.* "I'm sorry that this has to happen, but the decisions are made. We are going to provide assistance to you (*or* to each of the people affected)."

5. *What's the next step?* "I'm going to give you this letter outlining the severance arrangements. I suggest you take the rest of the day off and plan on being here tomorrow at 9:00 A.M. to talk with the benefits people. Also, we have engaged a very good outplacement firm, and I would like to introduce you to Fred Martin, who if you wish, will be working with you through your transition."

Classic (and Other) Questions

As stated earlier, this is not an interview in the traditional sense because its objectives are different. Essentially, it has three basic objectives: 1. to present unequivocally that "you no longer have a job here"; 2. to explain the conditions for leaving, that is, the details of checking out of the organization; and 3. to clarify the next step(s) in the termination procedure. It is fraught with emotion and trauma. There is a firing pattern that surfaces some basic emotions—anger, fear, self-pity and shock. One can add to those reactions some degree of disbelief that "it's happening to me" and in all probability, some bargaining attempts to negate or delay the decision.

Because every person is unique, everyone who is terminated reacts a little differently. They will ask a variety of questions, most of which will usually be defensive. So there is no single list of questions to offer that would cover all possible scenarios. However, there are a number of typical questions that seem to be raised with regularity in termination interviews, and these are outlined on the following pages with some suggested responses. All of the responses must be considered in terms of the particular circumstances of the organization and individual's situation, with due consideration for existing policies and procedures. The importance of planning and rehearsing the process cannot be overemphasized. It won't necessarily eliminate all of the problems, but should certainly minimize some of the dangers inherent in this difficult task.

Employee: Why me?
Manager: The decision was based on a thorough review of your performance; *or,* There is a cutback in staff and your job is being eliminated; *or,* There is downsizing as a result of the acquisition, and we will be doing

what we can to help you into a new environment where I'm sure you can be successful.

Employee: Why wasn't it Allen or Sandra?

Manager: I wouldn't have expected that you would agree with this, but as your supervisor, I have an obligation to communicate the decision to you and fill you in on some of the details/procedures involved.

Employee: This is a big/growing organization; there must be a place for me somewhere.

Manager: Before we made the final decision we crossed all the bridges, and we were not successful in identifying any other opportunity. So it is irrevocable . . . let's proceed with the other details.

Employee: Can't I have more time? It isn't easy to find another job.

Manager: I'm sorry, but it is final and is effective as of now. Now, I'd like to explain what the arrangements are so that you can move ahead with the task at hand.

Employee: You selected me because I'm (age, race, sex, etc.). didn't you?

Manager: That definitely is not correct. The reason is as I stated and for no other.

Employee: I want to see your boss (president, etc.)

Manager: I can't stop you from doing that, but I think it would be a mistake. I doubt that there is any positive value in it. As you know, this has been approved through channels in accordance with policy, so it is irrevocable. Let's turn our energies to the tasks at hand.

Employee: How am I going to break the news at home?

Manager: I think it's best to face up to it directly. I'm sure he/she will be supportive; and remember, we are going to assist with the transition to a new situation.

Employee: I think I'll institute a lawsuit.

Manager: I would give some real thought to that; obviously, it's your decision, but I would discuss it with a friend before I took that kind of step.

Employee: You know how much I know about our new products; someone will be interested in that.

Manager: Remember, you signed a secrecy/proprietary information agreement when you came to work. Also, it is important to remember that you will need references from the company, and violating that agreement would pose real problems on a reference.

Employee: What about my last performance review? You said I was doing a good job.

Manager: Conditions that existed at that time in the company have changed. We thoroughly reviewed possible options and arrived at this decision, which is irrevocable.

Employee: Just a minute—I want to record this so I get it straight.

Manager: If you wish to record this, we will have to reschedule so that I may have a Company attorney present.

Employee: When you hired me you said that with my background and experience, I would have a fine career here!

Manager: Conditions have changed dramatically, as you know, both organizationally and the direction the business is taking.

Employee: What about references?

Manager: The Human Resources Dept. will verify your compensation, dates of employment, etc., as per our policy. For more detailed inputs, you and I will work out the "party line." You may sign the Reference Release Form in order to allow us to provide more details.

Employee: I want to bring my attorney here to hear what you have to say.

Manager: You certainly can do that, and I will arrange to have a company attorney present.

Employee: I've forgotten more about accounting than you will ever know.

Manager: That's entirely possible and that should be helpful as you move into the job market.

Employee: If you let me go, your name/company will be on every hit list in the Department of Defense.

Manager: That's a risk we have to take, but I would give some considered thought to this point. That undoubtedly would paint a very negative picture of you.

Employee: Why can't I have a chance to turn things around?

Manager: We have considered all of the options and the decision is irrevocable.

Employee: Be honest with me; I need to know why this happened.

Manager: It is as I explained.

Employee: How will I ever find another job? I haven't looked for one in fifteen years.

Manager: We have arranged for professional job-hunting assistance through Avery Associates, a nationally known outplacement consulting firm. The plan is to have you meet with Bert Cleaver from that firm tomorrow morning.

Employee: Can I be rehired? Can I be redeployed?

Manager: You are eligible for rehire; however, at the present time, we are not hiring. The overall probability of rehire or redeployment is very unlikely, so you should concentrate your efforts on finding employment elsewhere.

Employee: Can I continue to work for a period of time?

Manager: No, we feel it is in your best interest and the company's for you to utilize your time exploring opportunities outside. The outplacement program is provided for that specific purpose.

Employee: How can the company do this to me after twenty years?

Manager: This downsizing, caused by business conditions, affected employees in every function. We considered a number of factors besides tenure—organizational requirements, skills, future requirements, performance among others.

Employee: Was Patty Brown terminated?

Manager: I really can't answer queries about other employees. I'm sure you can understand that.

In summary, because terminating people is such a negative process, it is pointless to try to make it positive with meaningless words, for example, "You are good and I'm sure you will find another job easily." Terminating probably doesn't get easier with practice, but practice may enable you to handle it in a more professional and humane manner. Above all, the manager should not get defensive, but approach directly and factually, not abruptly or in a condescending manner. The manager should avoid all platitudes and potentially discriminating remarks, and explain the next steps. The critical point to remember is that planning, brevity, and sensitivity are the keys to successful termination interviews.

4

A Manager's Perspective on the Psychology of Terminations

An Awesome Responsibility

Whether or not you as a manager have ever had to terminate an employee, it is a real and ever present possibility that at some point you will. The impact of a termination has far-reaching effects. If you as a manager are to meet your responsibility effectively, then the whole chain of events a termination may unleash must be understood. Managers must recognize all of termination's implications to be able to cope in a sensitive and humane manner.

The best way to anticipate termination problems is to understand the psychology of the impact. A number of individuals and viewpoints must be considered, and this chapter necessarily will discuss those viewpoints in detail.

Managers have always had to deal with terminations. Unfortunately, in recent years the problem has become more complex, because so many capable employees have had to be terminated. It is never an easy task to discharge someone, and it is infinitely more difficult when it is someone "who has done no wrong."

Managers' jobs have changed dramatically in the past few years for the same reasons that have resulted in so much realignment and restructuring of organizations. There is no end in sight for this volatility, so progressive organizations will ensure that their management develops the understanding necessary to deal with it. A major factor in that understanding will be comprehending the importance of work to the individual. Work is what gives meaning to a person's life. When change in an organization forces change onto people, they usually react negatively because they are concerned about themselves. There are few changes that organizations experience that are as disruptive as terminations, whether by the impact on the individual affected or on any of the other entities involved, for example, other employees, family, academia, local community, etc. Responsible managers understand the impact of terminations and the linkage that exists beyond just the individual directly affected. This is an awesome responsibility made more complex because the courts increasingly view a job as property. This highlights the "psychological contract" created when an employee is hired. This contract is based on the expectations of both parties, the company and the employee, and when these aren't met, the situation is often made more difficult through lack of understanding. The more an organization has to terminate, the more concern there must be about how it is done. This task has a great impact on the management responsibility spectrum, and like any management problem, it must be understood in some detail if it is to be solved professionally.

To best understand these responsibilities, the remainder of this chapter will be devoted to discussing the linkage that exists and the implications of the psychological contract.

As mentioned earlier, the terms used to refer to terminations tend to be so final, there is bound to be a negative psychology about the whole subject. Recent headlines offer further substantiation: "XYZ *Slashes* Workforce in Chicago"; "*End of the Line* for Many Employees at TAB Corporation." Other headlines and stories in the media indicate the severity of the impact of being terminated on some individuals: "Explosion Rocks Oil Distribution Plant" (Terminated Chemical Engineer Planted Explosives); "Man Leaps to Death from Building" (Controller Released in Restructuring); "Husband Wounds Wife, Two Children, Shoots Self" (Advertising Executive Released After Major Account Lost); "Executive Attacked in Company Lobby" (Administrative Assistant Released for Incompetence).

So, in the extreme, there can be irrational and violent reactions to terminations. It's all pretty funereal and deathlike; it is the end of a phase. Not surprisingly, many outplacement practitioners feel job termination may be more stressful than death. However, they also know losing a job is not the end; one must get on with life and career. Even though job loss isn't final in an absolute sense, it must be dealt with for a period of time. That requires communication about it with other people, which can be difficult. Since many people do not understand why this happens, they don't understand that in most instances, there's nothing "wrong" with the person affected.

It is very important for the manager to understand that few people comprehend the severity of reaction to termination until they are the victim. The reactions will range across the whole emotional spectrum, and no two people will react quite the same to being told they are terminated. It really is the ultimate criticism for most people, and that knowledge alone can cause sleepless nights and sweaty palms for the manager who must do the terminating, the "criticizer."

Regardless of the terminology we use or the degree of understanding that exists, there is no single reason why terminations happen. It is hard to pin down. Who is really at fault? It is seldom clear-cut or well defined. That's perfectly normal, yet everyone seems to be surprised when a terminated person reacts in any unorthodox manner. *All* parties to terminations experience some trauma and emotion, even if it is not directly expressed.

What the Psychologists Say

Most psychologists feel that people generally are very hard on themselves— they accept the blame for everything that goes wrong with their lives. Yet so many terminations today are ones in which the individual is completely blameless—a business is sold; a plant closes. But many people will still hold themselves responsible for what is obviously out of their control. As mentioned earlier, people are judged by what they do for a living. Jobs provide a psychological identity, as well as economic support for all of life's necessities. When a job disappears, it's not unnatural for an individual to blame himself along with the organization, and most certainly the manager. Most managers don't understand the whole range of emotions and reactions to be dealt with. They are not trained to cope in most instances, evidenced by the apparent dearth of orientation to even the mechanics of the termination interview in most organizations. This is not to suggest that all managers take psychology, but rather that they have some training to understand what really transpires in an individual's mind as he or she learns that "your services are no longer required." Then they will be in a position at least to suggest appropriate help.

Termination rebuts the unwritten agreement, the "contract" between employer and employee. Each had depended on the other, and now the agreement is broken.

If an individual is terminated who enjoys the job, finds it fun, challenging, exciting and in a good working environment (that's the kind of job everyone wants), they don't want to leave. The impact of termination will be that much greater than with the individual who perceives the job as a dull, boring, routine.

Because of the naïveté of most managers about the termination process, and the sympathy they may feel for the individual being terminated, there is an insidious danger—a tendency to compromise. In an attempt to ease the severity of the situation, for example, the manager says, "we have a project you can be helpful on as you phase out." Or, as Bill Evans did to Jim Manning in chapter 3, just blame it on the boss!

The Firing Manager

Why does the thought of terminating cause even the toughest manager sleepless nights? This is the same manager who can make significant decisions about large expenditures, new products, and so on. Faced with terminating, this same person gets sweaty palms and the shakes. A major reason for it is that personal as well as organizational relationships are involved. Varying degrees of attachment may form over time. A manager, in many instances, has a very difficult problem psychologically when faced with an individual termination. The individual might be someone the manager hired; may be a friend; someone the manager respects professionally; someone who has not performed inadequately. The reasons terminations are so difficult for managers are the following.

Terminations are as stressful as anything a manager does because they deal with something that has gone wrong. If something is wrong, who is to blame? "Maybe me, maybe the organization, maybe the individual!"

Terminations damage an individual's self-esteem because the road to success has been disrupted. People don't really want to hurt one another, and this hurts both parties.

Most terminations don't occur because of failure to do the job. It is a sign of the times that many competent and highly capable people are victims of situations completely out of their control, and that is difficult to face. It's almost always easier to terminate someone whose performance is unsatisfactory.

As does the terminated employee, the manager may experience some self-pity. Why do I have to be the one to do this? Maybe there is some alternative. Why do I have to play "God"? I'm ruining someone's career.

Robert North was a project engineer with Impel Electronics and a capable employee. Impel was forced by several factors to institute a cost-reduction program. Robert was one of the victims, and Tim Reilly, his immediate boss, faced the unpleasant task of informing him.

Tim thought highly of Robert, but there was no alternative. When he informed Rob of the decision, there was the usual reaction of shock, anger, etc.

As Tim spelled out the severance arrangements, he suggested to Rob that there was some project work that he could be helpful on as he looked for another job. Tim then went on to explain that Rob was to meet the next day "with Fred Boland of Callahan Associates, an outplacement consulting firm we have engaged. You need to get started with a job search and Boland is very good."

Rob met with Boland, and launched his job search. It was slow going as Rob was spending a good deal of time on the "project," and a number of planned job-hunting tasks were not completed with any urgency.

Boland questioned Rob's priorities, and the response was always "they have me busy on the project." Rob even mentioned to several coworkers that: "the project work just might be an avenue to continue with Impel. They really don't want me to go."

Meanwhile, both Tim and Dan Beck, the personnel director, regularly queried Boland about Rob's job hunting progress. Boland always reported, "It's slow because he is busy with Impel work." These comments had little impact, obviously, because after two months, Rob had developed very little job-seeking activity.

Tim's obvious guilt at having to let Rob go, and in trying to be a nice guy, made him commit a cardinal sin—keeping Rob involved. Robert, having the normal reaction of a terminated employee, felt logically "maybe they didn't really mean it." It gave him the opportunity to clutch at straws. In that frame of mind, Rob wasn't going to work very hard at his job search, but was going to prove his value to Impel, regardless of the termination message.

What a mess! An employee was to be released and provided assistance to find another job, but nothing went right. It is an impossible situation to make and effect a termination decision and then dilute it by keeping the terminee engaged on company work. It's a disservice to the company, the manager, and above all, to the individual, who may have a double dose of emotion and trauma when the truth dawns that it's "really over." When termination decisions are made, they must be final and irrevocable.

There is always a very fine line in all of this for anyone when they must do something as sensitive as terminating. The problem is having the proper amount or degree of empathy without expressing too much sympathy. The trick is that once the termination decision is made, there should be no reason to make the individual believe that you feel it shouldn't happen, but on the other hand, you can't be insensitive or too hard-nosed. It takes every ounce of professionalism to do this correctly.

The real emotion for the manager is in preparing for the actual termination. Most emotional matters anyone faces in work can usually be talked about to other people. With termination pending, it usually isn't fair or circumspect to talk about it, because if others know, it can cause other problems in the organization: the rumor mill gets cranked up! Yet another factor is that you, the terminating manager, know it's going to hurt the individual, because everyone works for a living, and taking someone's job away is tough.

The rationale for the termination may also have a good deal to do with the level of emotion the firing manager may experience. In other words, is it a termination for cause, or is it a termination without cause (caused by any of the economic/business factors discussed earlier)? A termination for cause may provoke several types of feelings. If, for example, the cause is a flagrant violation of rules or policy—something acceptable in terms of sound business practice—termination may be done with little feeling. The individual has knowingly violated acceptable rules of business conduct as prescribed by the organization. They are in the wrong and must leave the organization. This situation certainly eliminates most feeling that the individual is being compromised or taken advantage of; there will be little sympathy. This does not mean the termination should not be conducted professionally and within guidelines, but it means it can be done with more assurance that it is right and *has* to be done.

If it is a termination for performance or for political reasons (although seldom admitted), it will probably be more emotional and traumatic. The firing manager may assume some of the blame—"If I had spent more time with her, maybe she could have handled that project better," or "If I had worked a little harder with him on his interpersonal skills, perhaps we wouldn't be at this point."

Termination is never easy, but the burden is eased a bit when there is a specific policy-oriented reason or proven lack of performance. Matters deteriorate where termination is a question of politics—can't get along with the boss or others in the organization. This is harder to define into a specific reason that can be communicated to the individual, and so will cause more anxiety. The most difficult termination then, may be when it is in no way the individual's fault—not poor performance, politics, whatever. For example, the individual becomes redundant when the organization is acquired. The employee may be perfectly competent, loyal, productive, with high potential but circumstances beyond anyone's control dictate he or she is out! The emotional involvement of the firing manager ("I am hurting this individual; I am taking away her livelihood; I am hurting this person and his family; There but for the grace of God go I") will depend on the reason for terminating.

Whether we admit it or not, when someone or something that we have responsibility for fails, we feel it is partly our fault. Again, people are very hard on themselves, and in these situations, managers may overreact because of the sensitivity of the situation. It takes a strong, objective, honest and well-prepared person to deliver the termination message with the least emotion and the right amount of empathy, whatever the circumstances.

The Terminated Individual

As individuals, all of our lives and in our careers, we are trained, motivated and focused toward being successful and moving ahead by parents, teachers and employers. Talk is always directed to "moving ahead and moving up." Advancement is our culture; keeping up with the Joneses is the American dream. Television ads tell us to "be all you can be." We are not supposed to think of not being successful. It's an internal part of us to think and talk that way. However, there are times in any work life when there isn't enough attention, or perhaps preventive maintenance, by either employee or manager to avoid some career mishaps. Employees become overly dependent on the organization and the support systems supplied by it. A feeling of security develops, and maybe not enough attention is paid to their employment obligations. The employee does not think much about accomplishments, goals, what needs improving. This is particularly true in larger organizations which have historically provided security. Big-company employees often don't think hard about their responsibility to themselves. They tend to equate bigness with security, and that can be an insidious thing today, when job security as it used to be known is nonexistent.

It must be understood that when an employee loses that security and the attendant organization support systems, it is devastating and can be very lonely! Loneliness in this instance will be isolation, a lack of contact with familiar faces and places and things just when they are needed the most.

The Firing Pattern

Every person is unique, yet there is a common reaction of people when they are terminated. It is almost a standard set of reactions. The intensity of the reactions will vary, based on a number of factors, such as age, education, compensation, self-confidence, functional discipline. This reaction, the so-called firing pattern, is basically four reactions to the termination message: anger, fear, self-pity and shock. Gaining better understanding of each should help the manager gain a better perspective on this subject. Each of these reactions will also be influenced to some degree by Doctor Stybel's emotional and intellectual acceptance theory discussed earlier.

Anger is the first and possibly the most obvious reaction to being terminated. We can all get mad when criticized, and termination is probably the ultimate personal criticism. In its extreme, anger may be verbalized in terms of revenge or threats. The manager is truly the culprit in the terminated individual's mind.

Wayne Miller was the number two corporate purchasing agent at Emmert Corporation. Emmert was ripe for a takeover, and a deal was finally put together where Commonwealth Corporation purchased Emmert. After the usual two- to three-month honeymoon, Commonwealth announced a realignment of the combined organizations. This resulted, logically, in elimination of a number of redundant jobs, of which Wayne Miller's was one. Wayne's boss, Pat Ryan, with some orientation from the outplacement consultant engaged by Emmert, set up the scenario for the termination interview.

Pat called Wayne into his office on a Thursday morning and explained that he was going to be released in the upcoming realignment. He explained that all corporate functions were being impacted because of the number of redundant jobs as a result of the merger.

Wayne was angry: "How can you do this to me? I have been an excellent performer for years and supposedly was your heir apparent." He went on and on about the stupidity of the decision, the quality of management of Emmert, and a litany of other items. He ended his tirade by telling Pat, "You haven't heard the last from me. I'm getting a lawyer."

Pat remained calm and unemotional, and said all the right things in a very professional manner. He explained that in two days the outplacement firm would begin work and Wayne would be able to avail himself of their services. He truly felt sorry for Wayne, inasmuch as he was not a victim of anything he had or hadn't done. It was pure and simple duplication of jobs.

Wayne went back to his office and he was furious—in fact, mad enough that he dug into files and ran some of them through a shredder. Over the weekend, he talked to his brother-in-law, who was an attorney.

On Monday, Wayne, still angry, did keep his appointment with the outplacement consultant. They got along quite well, and eventually got around to discussing references. Wayne related the shredding story to the consultant, who explained to Wayne: "Never burn your bridges. Remember, you need them more than they need you at this point in time. Pat is your key reference, and if he isn't on board, it will be very difficult for you in the job market."

Fortunately, the consultant interceded and talked to Pat about being a reference. Pat agreed and told the consultant that Wayne, although his actions would cause some problems, did not destroy any critical documents. Pat understood that the emotion of the situation was what caused Wayne's reaction. Pat agreed to provide a good reference because he knew Wayne was a capable and professional person.

Happily, this situation ended on a positive note, but it is a real example of the type of anger that may surface, and usually with not as happy an ending.

George Fields, an engineer with VC Corporation, was terminated summarily one Friday afternoon. George was angry, but he also was tough, or at least put on a great macho face.

"Things" didn't bother George, and when his wife inquired about what happened and how he felt, he said "fine."

Several of his friends inquired, and George responded, "Hey, that's life; you win some and you lose some." VC Corporation provided outplacement for George and he used the same line with his counselor, convincing him that he was not upset.

It was about four weeks into George's search, and toward the end of a Friday afternoon session, George's counselor asked him, "Where are you going from here?" The counselor knew George had a place in the mountains, and assumed that's where he was heading.

George responded: "You want to know where I'm going? I'm going over to the office and punch that S.O.B. in the face."

This is a sad commentary, because the four weeks of counsel that he had received may have been wasted on George, who was really seething inside but wouldn't admit it and made no effort to get it out. The message is: better to blow the steam early than to waste time and potential job leads with hidden anger.

Fear is the second reaction to the termination message, fear of the unknown, of finding a new job. This exists with everyone, but may be more prevalent with older individuals ("no one is going to hire me. I'm fifty years old"). Age is only as big a detriment as a person allows it to be. Fear is also very ego-oriented with respect to the individual having to face peers, associates, and friends—"How do I tell people I failed?" Facing up to people is difficult, because most people don't understand why these things happen and as a result, they don't know how to react to the person terminated. It's like going to a funeral; what do you say after you say you're sorry?

Doug Beech was fifty-nine years old and a very capable chemist with a number of patents and inventions to his credit. Nevertheless, he was on the termination list when his employer was forced into a staff reduction. Even though Doug was well known in his field and had made many significant contributions, the decision stood. Doug was genuinely hurt—he had never worked anywhere else, and assumed he would be with the company until he was sixty-five. He was scared that this was the end of his life, so to speak.

Doug happened to have a friend, Larry, who was in personnel work. Larry talked through Doug's concerns about wanting to work and his concerns about "who will hire any one who is fifty-nine years old?" Larry knew that Doug would work somewhere, even if it was in a retail store. He had to be involved and have somewhere to go, or he would vegetate. Larry boosted Doug's self-confidence with the approach: "You can do anything you want to if you want to do it badly enough. Look at what you have accomplished over the years!"

Doug agreed; in fact, he stated: "As long as this (pointing to his head) is working, I want to work, and I do believe in myself. But I have really soured on big companies." Larry suggested exploring alternatives. Teaching was a natural outlet, and with Doug's knowledge and contacts, why not consulting? Doug today is teaching at a local university, and consulting 10-12 days a month in his field, with a small, up-and-coming, out-of-state company which is delighted to have his knowledge and expertise available to it in its formative stages. In this instance the fear was overcome, but it can be a very traumatic experience.

Michael Martin was an attorney, a cum laude graduate of a prestigious law school. Michael had never had a failure in his life; everything he ever did he did well. After graduation, he was hired as an associate by a top law firm at a premium salary. At the appropriate time that associates were reviewed and evaluated for partnership, Michael was informed he would not be selected, and that he would be wise to seek a position elsewhere. Michael was a basket case. Faced with his first failure, he was scared to death.

The firm offered the services of an outplacement consultant, and Michael reluctantly agreed to meet with them. The job-hunting process that they championed was heavily oriented to networking.

Michael was almost paranoid about networking his friends and associates. "I can't tell people I have been fired," he said, "I don't want anyone to know."

Lengthy explanations of the whys and wherefores of a job search failed to convince Michael of the need for assistance. It was suggested that some material be forwarded to him that he could peruse at his leisure. He was almost rude about that. "I don't want anything coming to me with the name of this company on it—suppose someone saw it?" He obviously needed some positive direction and help in facing the real world, but he refused the services offered and so informed his boss.

Michael's boss tried to convince him that it would be very valuable to have someone work through the job-hunting situation with him, but to no avail. The firm to this day does not know where Michael went or what he is doing, but they do know he has not joined any other local law firm.

Farfetched? Yes, but this form of fear can be devastating and completely ego-shattering. Pride can be self-destructive at times. Michael probably needed professional help even before he contemplated attempting a job search.

Self-pity, if not an immediate reaction to the termination speech, will surface at some point in the early phases of a job search. There will be a time when every terminee will voice at least to himself, "I can't be any good; I failed in this job." As stated earlier, we are often our own most severe critics and tend to blame ourselves for everything that goes wrong. Self-pity, unfortunately, often puts us in the frame of mind where we consider compromise.

Jean Roberts was a well-paid, experienced marketer with a good track record in three different organizations. However, Jean was terminated. She was angry, but had been through enough in her career to handle the emotion. She was a pretty tough lady and had worked very hard to get where she was. There was no immediate feeling of self-pity, because she had a good deal of confidence in herself and her abilities. She threw herself into her job search with all her determination and energy.

A couple of weeks passed and she had not had much positive response. In reality, there is no reason to expect that a new job will evolve in a few weeks; there are too many factors involved over which no one has control. It takes time to identify a job, make contact, be interviewed, have decisions made and an offer proposed. The time factor may be the most misunderstood piece of the job-hunting puzzle. But it is also the most difficult aspect for the aggressive, action-oriented person to deal with. It requires patience—a commodity in very short supply with most people.

The lack of positive, hard activity made Jean begin to doubt how good she was. She said to a friend, "Maybe I'm not that good and should lower my sights—maybe take less money." That's the self-pity syndrome promoting compromise.

Her friend said: "Jean, don't start that. If you are as good as everyone thinks, have enough patience to deal with the job-hunting process. You feel sorry for yourself because the phone isn't ringing off the wall. Your self-pity will cost you long range, because you will compromise, and that is bound to set your career back!"

Organizations will often take advantage of people when they lose self-confidence. They may propose a lower level position and a lower level of compensation. The person who compromises in his or her career seldom achieves long-range personal goals previously set.

Shock is the fourth reaction to termination. In some situations, this can be the most dangerous response, particularly in terms of physical and mental well-being of both the individual and his or her family. No organization wants to be or feel responsible for precipitating some physical or mental crisis. The termination checklist should identify at least some of the potential problems. The usual initial reaction of shock is: "You can't mean me. You must mean Susan or Joe. I'm better than they are!"

Termination is like a heart attack—something that always happens to the other guy. People can be employed in an organization that is dramatically downsized, and see friends and associates terminated, and still be shocked when their names are called. There is a level of disbelief, like a dream; "I'll wake up and it will be over."

Because shock is caused by disbelief, the employee may start bargaining, and the manager is Johnny on the spot! The person shocked by termination thinks there must be a way to "straighten out this misunderstanding." Terminations *must be* planned and orchestrated to be irrevocable; there should be no room for bargaining.

One more reaction can be added to the firing pattern: loneliness. It can be frightening in the context of finding another job, because job hunting is such an individual effort. Even though the effective job hunter uses all personal contacts wisely, one still may feel like an outcast, even a pariah. The support systems anyone in an organization is accustomed to, particularly the people contacts, often disappear. There is always some degree of concern on other people's part about guilt by association. Many people who were terminated have commented: "I felt like I had leprosy—people reacted like I was contagious. I was an undesirable person."

John Kruse was the ultimate fast-track young executive—bright, tough, with all the ego and self-assurance that required. At age forty-three, he was president of a $900MM division of Lindenauer Industries, and had been instrumental in turning the international operations around in eighteen months. John had worked all his life, starting at age nine in his father's store. He was an outstanding student, cum laude college graduate, and held a master's degree in business administration with distinction. He had had a meteoric rise in Manco Corporation, where he spent sixteen years, starting as process engineer and progressing to vice-president of operations. Hired away by Lindenauer, he was on the road to the top. If John had a problem, it was with his political skills—he had a penchant for saying what he believed. A refreshing, yet dangerous, characteristic. Several times during his early tenure at Lindenauer, comments were passed about nonbusiness items, some outside socially oriented activities, that went against the grain of several of the top executives, including the CEO. Nothing was said at the time, but it was a topic of discussion among the CEO and his key executives.

Corinne, the vice-president of communications, was the only person to raise the issue with John: "You don't understand the culture here, so be careful with your off-the-cuff method about outside activities, which are very important in this 'good old boy culture' we have!" No one else made any pretense of cautioning John, and on one occasion, he overreacted on the subject with a particularly derogatory comment. Shortly after this exchange, the CEO announced a restructuring that effectively eliminated the need for a divisional president. John was out. He was totally and completely devastated. He had never had a failure in his life, and now, like a bolt out of the blue, he was gone.

He retained, as part of his severance, all the accouterments of his office, such as secretary and limousine, but he learned the next day that he had lost something very important—a lot of his support. It was very apparent when he went to the executive dining room for lunch and no one would sit at the table with him. No one stopped by his office for a chat, and conversations stopped when he got on the elevator or walked down the hall.

John's comment to his wife summed it all up. "I feel like I'm naked and standing at the intersection of Forty-Second Street and Fifth Avenue at high noon."

Job Loss and Pride

Unfortunately, because John Q. Public tends to equate job loss with failure, it doesn't matter too much what caused the termination. What is critical is what happens with the individual who is terminated. It is not unusual for the individual to withdraw completely and not want to deal with anyone or confide in friends. That pride can be devastating.

As Ralph Williams, a former associate and experienced outplacement practitioner, puts it so aptly,

> the person terminated must accept the fact that a business decision has been made, and like it or not, it's irreversible. The issue always is Why? What happened? Countless, fruitless hours can be spent trying to sort out answers which may never be clarified. It's a double-edged sword—if the boss is completely honest, the terminee probably wouldn't agree anyway, and there

is always a tendency to become emotional and say something to be regretted later. So, in the final analysis, it may be better that the boss is "kind" in explaining why. This does not necessarily mean that one shouldn't raise questions to attempt to understand why what happened, happened, but always in the context that the information would be very helpful as one proceeds to seek another job. Ask in a professional and objective manner.[9]

The terminee must accept the fact that he or she has suffered a major loss and will have to allow a reasonable period of time to grieve, and within reason, to vent feelings. It is perfectly normal to be upset, but it must be set aside, because life must go on. The person must accept the fact that this change must be adapted to. It will be an emotional roller coaster—tremendous mood swings, high hopes and expectations, disappointments, rejection, high activity, and low activity. Williams summarizes: "The way to maintain balance and stability through this period is to understand it is a temporary, *not* a permanent state."

James Madison, an engineer, was supervisor of quality control at Arnex Gear Company, and one day was terminated from his job. He was a good performer, and although he would never be president, he was reasonably well thought of and well compensated, but Arnex was in a bind as the Germans had eroded their market dramatically. James had ten years with Arnex and was getting a fairly generous severance arrangement which would carry him for six months. Also, he was to have office space and clerical help available. James was shocked, and extremely embarrassed. A very proud man, he could not conceive of telling anyone close to him what happened.

He had, for years, ridden in a carpool with several neighbors to the nearby town where Arnex's operation was located. He gave absolutely no indication of his situation to his carpool. In fact, he was still at the corner every morning at 7:30 A.M. as always, and he was ready to go home at 4:30 P.M., just as he had for years. The carpool was not aware of his situation until he found another job and wasn't at the corner one morning. As a matter of fact, he did not confide in his wife until she became suspicious after several months. The job James accepted was an administrative job in the local hospital—less money, less responsibility; but he felt he saved face. He never recognized that being so stubborn that he felt he had to keep up the fake front for all those months really precluded him from making any extensive effort at a broad job hunt. He wouldn't follow up leads out of town, because he would have had to explain his absence. Sad story, but true. Pride overcame good judgment and continuation of a promising career.

Stress

So much of the psychological reaction generated by termination really relates to the unknown. For example, most people have not had to "look" for a job other than when they left school so have few skills and little knowledge about how to go about it. This fear or concern about what will happen often causes some degree of stress. Like *firing* and *termination, stress* is not a pleasant word, and it conjures up all kinds of different images in people's minds, including even the thought that maybe "he's a little wacko." Losing a job and coping with the often lengthy process of finding a new one can be one of the most stressful experiences anyone can have. Awareness of stress allows it to be dealt with, and we can relieve most of our stress if we are realistic and honest with ourselves.

There are many indicators of stress: some of the most common seem to be increased use of tobacco, drugs, and alcohol; insomnia; depression; overeating; back pain; irritability; and apathy. It is important when one feels increased tension, anger, fear, to relieve the symptoms before the problem(s) gets worse. There are certainly many techniques, but some of the most helpful are: discuss your problems—talk openly with family and friends; exercise—walk, play golf, whatever will take your mind off of your problem; eat a well-balanced diet; moderate use of tobacco and alcohol; practice your hobby, or start one—something to get your mind on a different track occasionally.

The objective is to concentrate on something else and to relax. Relieve the tension associated with the termination by involving yourself in other helpful and healthful activities. A former client of mine put a perspective on stress, which he had coped with admirably, when he said: "Don't be afraid to admit to stress. You don't need anything else that distracts from your self-confidence as you struggle to rebuild your career . . . and believe me, it shows and people will pick up on it. It's almost always a negative reaction." The bottom line for the individual may be understanding that he alone controls his destiny.

Women and Terminations

It is appropriate here to discuss the viewpoint and reaction of female employees to termination. Personal experience has indicated some factors to note to ensure a manager's most professional approach to terminating these employees.

The first point is that there is unfortunately still a great deal of prejudice and misunderstanding in the business world about women working. Many inequities still exist in the workplace.

1. More women work, and more women are assuming positions of increasing responsibility.

2. Women still earn less for comparable jobs. A 1987 study by Heidrick & Struggles, the executive search firm, indicated that on the average, executive women earn less—42 percent less—than their male counterparts.

3. Women, generally speaking, work harder to get ahead.

4. They tend to be measured (appraised) against the *best* in the organization, when others may be measured against the average.

5. As a rule, most women are concerned and sensitive about interpersonal relationships and have inherent perceptiveness about people. They may be more oriented to doing things the way all the new management books espouse—pay attention, listen, be concerned with everyone.

Women tend to have a more practical or pragmatic view of terminations in the sense that they have probably fought a lot of battles in the corporate world to get where they are. When the EEO laws opened more opportunities to women, that also logically made them subject to all of the problems and inherent risks involved in the world of work. Everyone is vulnerable to termination, regardless of who or what they are. So, even though the laws and organizational culture have not yet enabled achievement of total equality intended, the laws have, by opening the labor market to more women, achieved an equality in termination vulnerability: there *is* equal opportunity to be terminated.

There is probably just as much trauma and emotion involved for the woman, but it may not be as visible as with their male counterparts. Women may hurt more personally when terminated, because they probably worked harder to achieve what they have. They may also wonder when terminated, and perhaps logically, "Would I have lost my job if I were a man?" Experience shows that women generally handle fear, anger, self-pity, and shock, at least on the surface, better than men. This may be attributable to experience overcoming prior obstacles to get where they are.

Kirsten M. was a Ph.D. who had not only received several scholarships, but also had had several prestigious summer internships in government. She had served as an administrative assistant to a well-known senator, writing a variety of speeches and position papers for him. She had worked very successfully in a major bank, achieving a vice-president's title in a short period of time. She had a brillant and creative mind, as acknowledged by all who knew her.

An executive search firm contacted her about a position working for the CEO of a well-known, old line investment firm. Kirsten agreed and went through a series of interviews with various executives in the firm—none of them women. As a matter of fact, there seemed to be a dearth of women in the organization from her observations, and she had heard that they had a questionable reputation in their EEO activities.

The situation moved ahead rapidly and culminated in an excellent offer, which Kirsten accepted. Her responsibilities were closely tied to the CEO's activities and they worked together on a daily basis. She worked as she always had, very hard, and sixty-hour weeks were not unique. She was aggressive and spoke up in meetings, and a majority of her recommendations were accepted and put into practice. Several peers characterized her as a "breath of fresh air—tough, but bright;" but others were taken aback by her "brashness."

About six months to the day of her first reporting, the CEO informed his vice-president of personnel that Kirsten would have to go: "It just isn't working out. She doesn't act *like a lady*—she's a pushy broad. She doesn't fit in with our culture."

So, even in light of her apparent success and impact, Kirsten was in trouble. Would a man have had the same problems? Probably not, because he would probably be characterized as "hard-charging and innovative." She might have fared better also in an organization of younger generation managers, people more accustomed to dealing with someone like her throughout their education and careers. It's a different mentality than that which exists in many organizations still dominated by executives in their late fifties and early sixties.

The problems inherent in terminating women are not dissimilar from the same problems encountered with any of the "protected groups"—all of the manager's sensitivity, humanity and commonsense must be mustered to handle these situations professionally.

The Family

Another aspect of terminations is the family. This spouse role can be very difficult, particularly if he or she has not worked in a business environment and gained some understanding of the politics and subjectivity that influences many business decisions. Without some of that exposure, the spouse may have a whole different set of emotions to deal with. They may have more practical concerns—the children, the bills, etc.

The severity of termination may be greater for the spouse and family as it is usually difficult to comprehend how this could happen to someone they love and have faith and confidence in. This expression, however, usually turns to the positive: "How could they be so dumb as to fire him? What a loss for them!"

Bob Teigs was vice-president of marketing with Grocery Products, Inc. He had been with Grocery for fifteen years, so he was shocked when informed of his termination. His wife, Diane, and he had three children, a girl and two boys. The girl was to enter her freshman year at State University in a month or so; the boys were a couple of years away from college, and very active and talented athletes.

The day Bob was informed of his termination, he went home early and told Diane and suggested that he tell the children during dinner. Diane asked Bob how he felt about what had happened, and he responded, "I don't like it, obviously, and I'm not sure I really know why it happened, but I have to get on with my career, and we have to get on with our lives."

Diane countered with, "I think the whole bunch are lousy b–s." Bob was shocked; he had never heard Diane express such vehemence. She went on: "In spite of them, we will do okay, because I have confidence in you and your abilities. Something better will surface, but I will never, ever forgive them."

At dinner, Bob explained his situation, and of course the children were shocked and hurt that someone had done this to their dad. The two oldest children responded in a positive way. "What can we do? I can get a job rather than start college now. I can get a job after school and weekends to help out." Bob was overwhelmed. (The youngest, who had said nothing to this point, came up with a classic comment. "Dad, does this make you a free agent?" An interesting perspective.) Those reactions are not unusual; everyone is hurt because dad was hurt, but everyone wants to be helpful and supportive.

The dual-career family also experiences the same hurt and feelings, and they may also have some tough decisions about the next job and its location. The logistics are different with two careers involved. The priorities have to be sorted out.

One of the benchmarks of good outplacement counseling is involvement of the spouse. It will provide the spouse an understanding of why these things happen, what it takes to cope with the job-hunting process, how to look at finances, and how to cope with the stress. There are many stories about the impact of a termination on marriage and family, and often it can test these relationships to the extreme. It behooves the firing manager to keep in mind this often-overlooked aspect of terminating when faced with the task of releasing an employee.

The Organization

Expedience often outranks principle. Unfortunately the organization that faces group or individual termination often adopts that attitude. Terminating is something that doesn't suit the ego and the "gung-ho" attitude of most managements. It is often viewed as an impediment to progress, to moving forward. That's not always true, but psychologically, it's negative and goes against the ego of management because it implies something's wrong. The firing manager often has a sense of failure, and there may be a bit of this in the corporate conscience, also: "When something fails we are responsible for, maybe it's because we didn't do things right."

Also, there often is a management arrogance that says, "we understand everything better by virtue of who and what we are." "We know what's best" is an approach that often forces decisions in isolation, i.e. relative to terminations, not really understanding the hardships, emotion and trauma often imposed by terminations. To truly understand the implications of losing a job, one has to experience it. All the rules, policies and procedures that any organization has will never be able to convey all its implications to people not affected.

The psychological impact of terminations on the organization will be heavily predicated on the organization's beliefs, on its culture, its style of management, and its total attitude about employee relations. This will be reflected in the level of responsibility the organization will take for employees. The responsible organization accepts responsibility and imbues its staff with the philosophy that success depends on unity of the group, on trust, confidence and belief in others. The character of the organization is truly tested at times like these.

Just as terminating is an accepted responsibility of the manager, or he/she is not fulfilling the responsibility to the organization, the organization is not fulfilling its responsibility if it *does not want to terminate* those employees who are not contributors. The well-managed and productive organizations face this responsibility directly and professionally when necessary. That does not mean it's any easier or less of a problem, but a mentality must exist or be developed in the organization to make these decisions, regardless of how distasteful they may be.

So, the psychology of terminations, as applicable to the organization, is really reflected in how managers do their job in relation to the subject. The organization will be concerned primarily about the potential of litigation; the reaction of the communities of concern—the public, stockholders, customers, competitors, academia, etc.; and the most critical and vocal concern, the remaining employees. What will they think and who will they blame? Will they feel that they are still working for an organization with a future? They will need attention and communication, because even though they still have their jobs they may experience emotion and trauma. There may be some "survivor syndrome" and that can cause anger, fear, depression, and hostility. Don't let up on communication after the message is out; there must be follow-up to reassure.

The blame factor is important here also. Who's to blame? What went wrong? What did we do to make this happen? What could we have or can we do to prevent a recurrence? What will the marketplace think? What will customers think? The list is long, and all should be considered.

The organization always worries about coming off as the bad guy. "We are the people who made it happen—someone or something failed, and whose fault is it?" The organization may be embarrassed about the termination, concerned that it will reflect on them, that they will lose face.

The organizations that will best cope with terminations are the ones that understand the no-fault concept stated by Jim Gallagher, as part of their culture. People still want the same things in their jobs—confidence, respect and recognition from their supervisors and coworkers, in addition to equitable compensation. When the individual loses the confidence of the boss, for whatever reason, both parties, the boss and the employee, recognize that the worst thing for both of them and the organization is to continue the relationship. This is becoming an accepted fact of life because it makes so much sense. Gallagher goes on to say that a work situation is primarily a relationship, as is marriage. Just as it is socially acceptable now to bail out of a crashing marriage, so it has become managerially acceptable to terminate a failing work relationship. This trend underscores the fact that terminations are prompted by incompatibility more often than incompetence. As a result, the increasing frequency brings greater acceptance. They occur more often and for a variety of reasons, and also because of more open and candid performance appraisals, which allow both parties to make meaningful decisions.

The work relationship, much like a marriage, depends to a great extent on the chemistry, the interpersonal relationship. When that erodes or disappears, there is probably only one solution. It is also probably true that neither party to the failure thinks he or she was the cause. In most instances neither party is 100 percent to blame. There are two sides to every story, and when both parties to the situation think they are blameless, it is better for them to split. It is better, regardless of who's right or wrong, because neither party really wants to perpetuate a situation with the other person.

To take that thought one step further, when an individual gets hurt in an organization, all the rest may suffer to some degree. They may be suffering through a period of unrest and personal concern: "What's going to happen to me?" "When is the other shoe going to drop?" It may be concern about the future vitality of the organization. The organization must understand that, and be aware of all the implications of terminations. It must be able to react with professionalism and dignity, not just ignore the problem.

The organization must understand the psychological impact of firing on both the employees and the firing manager in order to fulfill its obligations. That obligation is not only the organization's side of the employment obligation, but also to respect the employee's dignity, regardless of the employee/employer relationship.

The World

Terminations have impact on everyone in the organization. However, there is another, often-overlooked sphere of influence in terminations: the outside world, that is all of the communities of interest. They each have an impact on the organization; sometimes subtle, but always important. This is regrettably not understood by many organizations; because in their naïveté (or arrogance), they don't feel they have to tell anyone—"It's our problem and we will handle it how we want to."

The world, right or wrong, will view termination as a negative. There is little understanding yet of the whys and wherefores of people losing jobs. Whether thinking of the individual or the organization, termination implies something wrong. Someone or something is at fault.

Stockholders

In relation to termination, the stockholders may well be in the same position as the remaining employees. They, like the employees, have a real stake in the future of the organization. They will be waiting to see what happens next. They wonder if something is wrong with the management team; what they can look forward to in the future; whether the organization will remain viable and profitable; if their money is safe.

The stockholders have confidence in the organization, or they probably would not invest their money in it. They have to be concerned when something goes wrong. They deserve some answers and will need reassurance, just as the remaining employees will.

The Community

Whatever the organization's credibility in the community, terminations can erode that credibility. It is often said that the biggest critics an organization has when terminating employees are the employees who remain. If that is true (and it seems to be), then the second most critical group may be the community in which the organization exists. The best intentioned, most supportive (for example, United Fund, community projects) organization can be condemned if it seems to be anything other than professional and sensitive to terminees. The word gets around quickly and if the organization is not a good communicator, all the good work and intentions may evaporate. The impact of terminating may involve multiple locations and multiple communities, and regardless of how it is handled, it is a fact that it will have some impact everywhere in the final analysis. Honest and direct communications will pay real dividends—remember, rumors are always worse than the truth.

Academia

The reaction of academia to an organization's termination woes will depend on the degree of mutual involvement. Colleges and universities not only are the suppliers of future manpower, but in many instances are also providers of a wide variety of research in all functional areas. Above all, they can influence perceptions of an organization, particularly among students, both undergraduate and graduate, and also the general public. Keeping the campuses informed solidifies the relationship and provides insurance for the future.

Potential Employees

This sector encompasses both new graduates, as well as others who may be potential job candidates at some point. The reaction of most people to hearing of an organization's terminating people is, "that must be a bad place to work." Organizations with a reputation for continual turnover are always suspect—either they are poorly managed or they hire bad people (usually one and the same).

The impact on potential employees will also depend on how terminations are handled, how they are perceived in the "marketplace." When organizations do a creditable job with terminations, when they are a caring organization, it may well remove the onus associated with the firing. Psychologically, it can be a big plus because it makes them appear honest to the outside world.

Summary

In summary, the degree of psychological impact on the individual, the organization, the family, etcetera will be a direct result of how professionally, efficiently and effectively the termination is handled. If it is done well, there will be a faster recovery from the shock and more positive feeling for all concerned. If done poorly, there will only be negative feelings, emotion, a tarnished reputation, and maybe litigation. Therefore, it behooves the manager to understand all the details outlined in this chapter. No termination is isolated!

5

The Manager's Guide to Avoiding Terminations' Pitfalls

It's Not What You Do, It's How You Do It

The old adage of terminating is "it isn't what you do to the individual but *how* you do it." People file wrongful discharge lawsuits because of *how* they were treated at the time of termination. Some 22,000 suits were filed in 1987; so it should prove that proper planning and execution of terminations is of the utmost importance. A major reason there is usually little humanity, sensitivity or feeling of responsibility shown toward people being terminated is the maze of legalities and technicalities that have to be considered. The result often is that terminating is done by rote ("you can't be very nice when everyone wants to sue"). The *how* is what impacts all the parties to the termination, all those in the linkage. The way a person is terminated is the standard by which those remaining will judge the organization. If terminations are done with care and concern, there will be respect for the organization. When terminations are done with care and concern, the anger and emotion will be of a lesser degree—*how* you treat people almost always determines the extent of their anger. The *how* is the next reflection of the humane and professional approach explored in this text. *How* it is done will be a major factor in how many self-inflicted wounds the practicing manager and the human resources manager incur. When managers understand and fulfill their responsibilities, few of the wounds are likely to be serious.

Handling terminations correctly means avoiding self-inflicted wounds like those in the following termination scenarios. It would be difficult to measure the anger and the emotion caused by these thoughtless approaches.

Temple Computer Services Inc. had been working straight out on a major project, weekends and nights. On a balmy Friday at noon, the six key project people went out for a well-deserved, leisurely lunch. Upon their return, there was an urgent staff meeting arranged, and the six were informed that Corporate had received instructions that the project was canceled and they were being terminated. They were told to clean out their offices by 4 P.M. and to report back Monday 9 A.M. for specific details. When they left the meeting, several uniformed security guards were in evidence as they cleaned out their offices.

Even though the individuals eventually got generous severance, and so on, the anger persists to this day. The abruptness of the announcement, the timing (Friday afternoon), and most of all the presence of the security guards—"we felt like convicted felons"—all added up to very negative reactions from those departing and especially from the survivors. Within a month several other key members of the staff left Temple. One commented, "I don't want to work in a police state."

An able and effective university administrator at a school with a newly hired president returned from lunch one Friday to find a note card thumbtacked on his office door. It read: "Would appreciate it if you would clean out your office by the end of the workday. You have been replaced and the personnel officer will expect you Monday at 9 A.M. to discuss details. [signed] _____, President"

The president of a large division of a major U.S. manufacturer was summoned to the chairman's office late one afternoon. As he entered the office, the chairman held up a piece of paper and said, "This is a letter from one of your employees that states that you are an insensitive manager, so I will be letting you go." Then before the amazed president could respond or react, the chairman quoted from Shakespeare to the effect that "all's well that ends well."

A marketing manager's position was part of a staff reduction due to relocation of an office. On the day of the announcement to the staff, several meetings were scheduled for the morning with exempt staff, and one in the afternoon for nonexempt personnel. The morning meeting took place, and the marketing manager heard all the details. She attended the afternoon session and was shocked to realize it was for nonexempt staff—She should have been with the morning group. When she questioned the vice-president of personnel, he admitted a mistake; he had told his secretary to arrange the meeting "to get all the girls in, in the afternoon." Little thought to the details resulted in a very upset employee, and compounded the bad feelings already present.

A director of manufacturing's boss stopped in one morning unexpectedly. He handed the director a lengthy memo which detailed organizational changes, including a significant downsizing of the manufacturing operation and a new job for the director with less responsibility. "Why don't you read this through?" he said. "I'm off to a meeting and I'll be back in an hour and a half, should you want to discuss it."

A large corporation with a number of regional offices was forced into some significant staff reductions, which resulted in the closing of several of those offices. An outplacement firm was engaged. On the morning of the internal announcement of the reduction and the introduction of the outplacement consultants, an employee brought in a copy of the company magazine, which headlined "Company reports record earnings for first half of year." That's great timing!

Management (In)competence

For many organizations, avoiding some of the pitfalls or wounds may require a change in management philosophy. So much of what goes wrong relates primarily to management competence (or incompetence), the culture of the organization, and how it is managed. Chapter 6, "Control & Training," will elaborate many points to be made in this chapter. The activities that will avert pitfalls are necessarily very closely related between the practicing manager and the HR manager.

Peter F. Drucker in *The Practice of Management* said: "The manager is the dynamic, life-giving element in every business—the quality and performance of the managers determine the success of a business, indeed they determine its survival. For the quality and performance of its managers is the only effective advantage an enterprise in a competitive economy can have."[10] In view of this, why does business persist in the belief that a person can be anointed a manager?

It is generally assumed by most people that because managers have a responsibility to manage, they are more intelligent, perceptive and different from the rest of us. To most people, management represents success, so the assumption is made that they must know how to do things right; managers are looked up to, so the assumption is that they must be better; managers are infallible; managers have real concern and commitment for the organization. The point here is that no one person is really perfect or that much better. Managers are not born, they are made. Organizations cannot continue to assume that having a manager's title means that you know how to manage. Training and orientation is needed just as surely as there is for any other function or task in the organization. Without training and direction, a manager is no different from anyone else except by title.

Terminating is a distasteful but most necessary task for a manager. Because of the complications involved today, there must be a greater awareness instilled if that responsibility is to be carried out in the manner it should be. The necessity is very clear: keeping someone in a job when he or she is not competent or suitable is wrong. It is wrong for the person; it is wrong for peers, subordinates, and supervisors; above all, it is wrong for the organization. An organization's future hinges on its people assets!

In *Supervision—The Management of Organizational Resources,* Durand and Schoen state that "a key skill good managers have or must acquire is to understand the differences and similarities in human personality and the needs, attitudes and perceptions of people."[11] They go on to say that: "managerial effort is directed toward accomplishing productive work by organizing and motivating the efforts of other people. In our society managers are also expected to create the type of work climate that will enable subordinates to achieve their personal goals and a sense of satisfaction from the work."[12]

"A manager is a manager because we said so" is a very bad assumption. Highlighting this is the belief by many students of management that managers do their poorest work in the hiring, appraisal, promotion, and termination of people. Those are all things we assume they do well because they are managers.

The past few years have seen more questions raised publicly about management competence, as evidenced by the onrush of publicity and action contemplated by various groups such as the Council of Institutional Investors (CII). Some unusual changes have already occurred, as stockholders and employees have criticized management and its mistakes. In 1987 General Motors made some significant policy changes in response to criticism from both stockholders and employees—certainly a first in the automotive industry!

We may be on the threshold of sweeping changes in attitudes about how businesses are managed. Terminations have been a particularly sensitive subject with many stockholders, and particularly employees, who have seen cost reductions and resultant restructuring, for example, affect coworkers (with sometimes minimal assistance in coping with job loss emotionally and financially). On the other hand, they see management, who may have brought about the situation, cushioned by generous golden parachutes as they face job loss themselves.

The psychology of management will also change in a more positive way when there is more recognition in American industry that the obsessive and continued focus on quarterly earnings seems to prevent any really meaningful long-range planning, and thus, in many instances, meaningful growth or real productivity. There "isn't time" to do the necessary things. This is particularly true with people aspects. Many organizations have been so overly reactive to what in many instances they have brought on themselves through shortsightedness and mismanagement, that they erode the biggest and most important asset they have—people. At the first sign of trouble in the business, the decision is made to "get rid of x people," and usually with little thought about the consequences, either short or long term. There may be many ways to deal with the problem other than cutting the payroll. Organizational components should also be scrutinized. How is it structured and managed? What is the organization's productivity quotient? These decisions should require some thorough analysis: What do we need to continue to do? Maybe this is a product problem, a marketing problem, et cetera. This is not to imply that being a manager in a world fraught with litigation isn't difficult, because everyone wants everything written down and spelled out in infinite detail.

Leadership, or management, is two things: intelligence and integrity. Leadership, or lack of, never shows itself more than when in a crisis. In an organization, it will be truly tested when there are termination problems. Good leadership also means managing in a rational and sensitive manner.

To deal with any type of problem in an organization, management must understand the complexity of the problems. To understand and to be able to cope effectively, managers must be trained.

Since we think managers are different and smarter, it is too often assumed that training is for others in the organization, because they need it. The success of an organization in dealing with a specific problem (in this case, terminations) will depend on how well managers are trained and oriented to their responsibilities.

The Linkage Problem—Hiring to Firing

Terminations are inextricably linked to the total people process in any organization. The human resources function (the people function) is concerned with six areas, identified by Wayne Cascio of the University of Colorado:

1. *Attraction*
   a. identifying job requirements;
   b. determining the numbers of people and the skills mix necessary to do the jobs; and
   c. providing equal opportunity for qualified candidates to be considered for jobs
2. *Selection*—the process of choosing the people who are best qualified to do the jobs
3. *Retention*
   a. sustaining employee motivation to perform jobs effectively; and
   b. maintaining a safe, healthy work environment
4. *Development*—preserving and enhancing employees' competence in their jobs by improving their knowledge, skills, abilities, and other characteristics (KSAOs)
5. *Assessment*—observing and evaluating attitudes relevant to jobs, job performance, and compliance with organizational personnel policies.

6. *Adjustment*—providing services, such as retirement counseling and outplacement, which are intended to maintain the required number and skills levels of employees.[13]

These functions can be carried out at the individual, group, or organizational level. Sometimes they are initiated by the organization (for example, recruitment efforts, management development programs), and sometimes they are initiated by the individual or group (for example, voluntary retirement, safety improvements). Moreover, the functional responsibilities are highly interrelated.

The linkage of the termination process really starts before hiring; it starts when realistic job specifications are compiled to define what is needed to perform successfully in that particular part of an organization. Selection must then be done with the level of objectivity that ensures that a given job candidate can and will do the job, i.e. that the "right chemistry" exists. Then comes orientation which, if not conducted with the attention it deserves, may be the beginning of the end. Appraisal involves defining the future for the individual, either internally or externally. Termination is necessitated by failure to perform, or when other factors interfere with the individual's career.

Because people are the key asset in any organization, their care and feeding is crucial to its survival. Understanding that one step feeds on the other, you must go back to the basics when little attention is given to each and every aspect of the people process. Terminations would not be so prevalent nor so studiously avoided as an unpleasant task if more thought was given to "why." Why are we at the point of terminating? What went wrong? Where did I (or the system) fail? What do we need to improve in order to minimize the problem in the future? This linkage problem can be put in a good context by ensuring that the organization understands that human resources is everyone's responsibility. Responsibilities can no longer be abdicated by saying "that's Personnel's problem"; that just won't wash anymore. A high priority for anyone in charge should be to get rid of the line between the practicing manager and the HR department. Every manager must understand he or she is at least partially HR Manager. Managers have the real responsibility for hiring, training, appraising, and terminating—that's what makes them managers. That's why they get paid more.

To avoid serious pitfalls, the organization must ensure that no manager is allowed to procrastinate in any termination situation to the detriment of the individual in question, the organization, and the other employees. It just isn't fair to any of them. The problem often starts at the beginning. I have often said that fired managers often feel like incompetent failures. They worry about pulling themselves together and building a solid career elsewhere. Often, however, whether they know it or not, the responsibility for their firing isn't the manager's alone. Bosses who fail to screen adequately applicants for roles, or who fail to give subordinates "timely, honest and accurate evaluation of . . . progress on the job" are setting others up for failure.[15]

Managers who will have to face the trauma and humiliation of firing should remember that failing in one endeavor doesn't make a person a failure. Some people, in fact, discover their true calling only after being forced out of positions that never suited them.

Really successful organizations have managers who understand that one of their major roles is to train subordinates in all respects, including honest, objective appraisals of how they are doing. These organizations measure their managers on their skills and abilities to work with and develop the potential in employees. Well-trained managers will do *all* aspects of their jobs better, and as a result should certainly handle terminations in a more positive manner.

Perhaps one of the best things any organization can do, then, is to ensure that its managers are well trained in *how* to train, motivate and develop subordinates to reach their full potential. Again, as discussed earlier, managers are looked up to and should be prepared to provide direction, inspiration and motivation. Training should be focused on them for that reason. For example, a manager trained in interviewing techniques will probably have a good selection process in his/her part of the organization, and will ensure that those techniques are passed along to subordinates.

The Procrastinating Manager

Although the organization may be at fault through lack of managerial competence, the day-to-day problems are best reflected in the *Procrastinating Manager*. The real wounds are inflicted by them. The procrastinating manager is the individual who perpetuates losing situations by failing to take the necessary action. This is a manager who knows there is a problem with an individual or individuals, but will always find a way to justify not taking the inevitable action. Many will never resolve this until forced to, and at times, they may still take the easy way out by blaming someone else for the failure, or will even pass the problem along, which is the worst kind of procrastination.

Bert Crosby was terminated by Rite-Flex Corporation after ten years and a succession of jobs in various parts of the organization. The jobs Bert held were, on the surface, increasingly responsible, and he had moved through the organization, which generally would be viewed as a factor of success. Don Swift, the outplacement counselor engaged to work with Bert, was intrigued by the circumstances as initially presented—an individual with an apparent record of progression at Rite-Flex. As Don worked with Bert and became more familiar with his background and the Rite-Flex organization, he became more curious and suspicious about Bert's demise. One afternoon while visiting Rite-Flex, he met Bert's original boss, Scott, who was also the hiring manager. In the ensuing conversation, it became apparent that Scott felt Bert should never have been hired by Rite-Flex, but that the exigencies of the moment made it happen. In fact, Scott admitted: "I gave up on Bert shortly after I hired him. He should have been terminated then, but I arranged a transfer for him hoping that he might change, and he has been passed around the organization ever since, but has never really proven himself." Sad, but true. No one would face up to this mismatch for ten years! What a disservice to Bert, who now was ten years older and in the job market. Perhaps he should have taken the initiative, but with a succession of moves, it was easy to assume that things were fine, that the organization was taking care of him. It was a failure of management and a disservice to the organization to have had for ten years the expense and concern about what to do with Bert.

Another mark of procrastinating managers is not admitting they can't work miracles. Managers often say: "Let's go ahead and make an offer, even though she's not a perfect fit. I can change her when she comes in here to work." People don't change, really, and organizations are littered with employees who someone thought could be changed.

Another good example of procrastination is Frank White from chapter 3, who knew he had to terminate Jane Green but tried to pass off the responsibility to someone else. That is not only procrastination but also abdication of a primary managerial responsibility.

Nothing works well in an organization without the full and visible support of all levels of management. All the good intentions, policies, rules, and pronouncements mean nothing if responsible managers are not involved in every phase of the particular process. For any organization to face realistically the problem of terminations today with complications like employment at will, there are some basic concepts that must be understood. For example, the turnover of people, for whatever reason, is not necessarily all bad, nor is it always bad that people leave the organization who the organization doesn't *want* to have leave. If the environment or chemistry isn't right for them then they should leave before they become dissatisfied and unproductive and possibly disruptive. It may be a no-win situation for both parties. Organizations who pride themselves on never losing or never terminating people may be cheating themselves and their stockholders of potential unrealized earnings.

However, there may be failure in *both* instances—where there is turnover and where there isn't. Saul Gellerman raised a very interesting point: "Something may be wrong with a company that suffers too little turnover during an economic boom. Why are its employees not attractive to other employers?"[14]

There is a growing recognition that manpower problems work both ways, in and out, and organization policies increasingly reflect that. Unfortunately, the lack of definition, planning and follow-through in so many organizations vis-à-vis people programs has forced learning the hard way, evidenced by the chaos in some industries over the past few years caused by foreign competition. It is increasingly clear that change keeps organizations vital: it opens up new opportunities and allows for the introduction and development of new ideas; it provides the incentive for individuals to improve and broaden themselves. No one is "long term" anymore, and if people programs are managed correctly, they will facilitate getting the right people into or out of jobs at the right time. That's what managers must understand!

Don't allow yourself to be a procrastinating manager which really means management by guilt; that approach hurts everyone. Procrastinating managers string everyone along—themselves, their employees, and the organization—to everyone's detriment.

Learn to Be a Good Manager

Know Yourself

To avoid being a procrastinating manager, you must learn to cope with the complex problems businesses face today. The primary question always relates to people—most importantly, how to deal with people in an environment when there is less opportunity for promotion, when loyalty to the organization is not a top priority, and the necessary commitment must be instilled through actions and beliefs. Galileo once said, "You cannot teach a man anything, you can only help him to find it within himself." Management development is really self-development; and we do need to train people to be leaders.

Managers should, as should everyone periodically, do some reflective, introspective thinking about themselves. This requires honesty, objectivity, and facing up to weaknesses, biases and prejudices. Once you as a manager recognize these, you will be better able to deal with them, and to make good decisions in spite of them. Face up to your managerial-style shortcomings. Assess your strengths; understand your pluses, skills, and abilities. This exercise will help you meet your basic responsibilities as a manager; by learning how to manage yourself, you will be much better prepared to manage others. Take every opportunity to hone your management skills. It is very important to learn as much as you can about how and when to make changes and difficult decisions about people. Remember, the most poorly performed managerial tasks are usually hiring, assessing, and terminating. Learn as much as possible about the three major responsibilities: managing your function/business; managing your managers; and managing your employees. Work at managing so there is no incompetence. A primary responsibility of management is to get rid of noncontributors (people or functions). Understand the dangers of organizational bureaucracy, and what "lean" really means—shedding incompetence and paying more attention to the important things.

The wise manager devotes a good deal of time to hiring, developing, and promoting people. For example, good hiring practices will get the right person in the right place at the right time. The "right" person is the one who is best qualified to do the job, not someone who is overqualified, or underqualified. Hiring the wrong person costs a lot of money—hiring costs, training costs, terminating costs. The more senior the hire, the more it will cost.

Learn to Appraise Effectively

For a manager, the second-most avoided task is performance appraisal. Although not the emotional confrontation that a termination might be, appraisals as practiced in most organizations have a negative aspect. It's the time for criticism and criticism is not easy to give or receive. Regardless of the fear of appraising, there is no choice but to do them and do them well. They may be the critical documentation in termination, and constitute your "case" should you have to go to court. They may be crucial to your decision should your organization be faced with a downsizing and you have to decide who goes and who stays!

To conduct effective performance appraisals, don't allow your own blindness to impact your judgment. In conducting appraisals, most managers aren't aware of their shortcomings; they are not a panacea and there will always be mistakes. Evaluation of human beings by human beings is bound to be fallible. More wounds are inflicted when people try to change people to conform to their own standards. Learn that appraisals are *performance* appraisals, and not *potential* appraisals. When you begin to fantasize about potential it often becomes real, and it really can't be that factual. One of the most valuable management skills is the ability to identify strengths. It is a crucial skill for good management, because that's what an organization is built on. Be willing and able to give credit for what people can do. Recognize that, while weaknesses may be easier to spot, you don't build an organization on them.

Performance appraisals work best when there is not a structured schedule of periodic formal sessions. Conducting appraisals as needed always works better because people know where they stand. Well-managed organizations do continual evaluations. If everything is done "by the book," it usually isn't productive—free and open communication between management and employees breeds success. Just like terminating, a manager must be able to perform this aspect of the job in a responsible manner. Failure to conduct effective performance appraisals does a real disservice to employees, and also jeopardizes the future of the organization.

You will need all your interpersonal skills for this task. Employees have a right to know how they are doing, and they need to know, just as you need to know to be an effective manager. Lack of open and honest discussion can affect performance, and then everyone will suffer.

To develop the proper attitude about the value of appraisals, you must think of every employee as an asset, and therefore his/her performance and contribution to the organization must be evaluated periodically. Without true measurements of this asset, the organization will not be able to utilize it effectively.

Consider these summary facts about performance appraisals:

No one is perfect, nor can you expect them to be.

As manager, you should approach this task in a positive frame of mind: What can my people really do? Spend less time worrying about what they can't do.

When you really know strengths, you know better how to spend time, how to utilize people.

Appraisals should be continual. The specifics of any discussion must be written down.

If a person's performance is not acceptable, then it's the manager's responsibility to communicate that message, and act on it.

"Thank You" Management

I have long been a proponent of what I call "thank you" management. Because most employees never hear a positive word, there is amazing benefit from saying "thank you for contributing"; "thank you for working so hard"; and above all, "thank you for trying." The word gets around that you appreciate positive efforts, and employees will seek that reinforcement through performing as well as they can. People never forget praise, and will respond in a positive way to your direction as a result of it. Performance appraisals are more effective, because people know where they stand on a continuing basis. This technique is worth a try, and it doesn't cost a nickel—it's just two words.

Who Should Go?

While seldom completely objective, the decisions about terminations are in some ways easier to make when a staff reduction is planned. Though still difficult, it is often easier to deal with a group of people where "it's no one's fault . . . we are in this together." When faced with the reality of multiple terminations, how should you decide which employees are to go? This may be one of the hardest decisions, but it must be made as objectively as possible. Deciding who should go should ultimately be done by the operating unit of the organization, not corporate management (although they may dictate a percentage reduction). If specific decisions about "who" are not line decisions, the organization's credibility may suffer. If top management makes all the decisions, this may compromise manager's authority; when that happens, people often take sides, and that can be disastrous. No one knows your organization better, so you must have the responsibility, or you aren't "the manager."

These decisions must obviously be guided by policy and specific criteria, with particular sensitivity to any potential affirmative action implications—if you attempt to use *different* termination selection methods for any protected class (such as minorities, females, or employees 40–65 years of age), you run some real risks. Above all, do not let seniority become the prime criterion. Your newer employees may be women and/or members of minority groups. Therefore, make every effort to avoid the last hired/first fired syndrome. Unfortunately, the usual criteria for terminations reflect the crisis atmosphere that probably provoked the terminations. Outlined below are these "crisis criteria."

1. *Seniority.* This is generally viewed as the fairest criterion, particularly in organizations unionized by contract or in government. Its primary characteristic is length of service, not contribution. In a sense, it may be counterproductive to the whole objective.

2. *Performance.* If this has not been precisely defined and *carefully appraised*, it may prove a poor criterion. How good is your appraisal system?

3. *Past contribution.* Unfortunately, this is often just past history, and the decision to retain becomes merely a reward for prior performance.

4. *Future contribution.* This is probably an effective criterion only when a good inventory of personnel exists so that some assessment of overall talent is available to make a judgment based on future business needs.

5. *Overhead people.* An immediate solution is to cut the non–profit-and-loss functions. This is too often done without considered thought, and often has devastating results.

6. *Percentage reduction.* A reduction of specific operations must be made across the board. This criterion seldom, if ever, gets to the real crux of the problem.

Points 5 and 6 are really essential to any plan involving the release of a number of employees. If faced with a multiple termination problem, you must determine whether the reduction plan is tactical or strategic. If strategic, what part of the business or function can the organization do without? If tactical, it may mean to cut the payroll by a specified percentage. Whatever the approach, do not lose sight of the fact that too much concentration on organizational components may detract from a real opportunity to remove redundant jobs!

Organizations vary greatly in terms of product line, technology, etc., which may be a major factor in the priorities in any staff reduction, but managers must determine the most realistic criteria to fit their organization's particular problems, and they should be outlined *before* a reduction is imminent so it can be accomplished with the proper thought.

Assuming that your organization has a realistic performance and appraisal system, the following may be good selection criteria:

1. *Employee's discipline*—Is it "in-demand" training? What will be the demand a year from now?

2. *Program on which employee works*—What is the program's priority in the organization's long-range plans?

3. *Performance appraisal*—Where does the employee rank vis-à-vis others? (There may be times when managers have no poor performers, which makes item 4 below the key performance criterion.)

4. *Appraisal of potential*—What impact will the loss of the individual have upon the organization in the future?

5. *Specific expertise*—Does the individual possess specific or unique expertise that is not obtainable elsewhere within the company?

6. *Experience in general*—Is the combination of expertise and exposure the individual possesses so unusual that its loss cannot be compensated?

7. *Overall capability*—Where will the individual rank in terms of other criteria/other individuals being considered?

Even the best systems for developing criteria for a reduction require some soul-searching and hard decisions. Sometimes it may be difficult to maintain objectivity, but the task will be significantly easier if you have done effective and realistic performance appraisals.

It will also be extremely helpful to have a continuing review process for the organization's and your objectives. This will provide you with answers about certain of the criteria at any given time. Regardless of how effective the selected criteria may be, they should be reviewed after any reduction is consummated. A review should prove invaluable in preventing future mistakes. The best way to handle any termination(s) is to prepare for it with a little preventive maintenance. Without this ounce of prevention, you may utilize the wrong criteria and make poor decisions in selecting those who go. Criteria should be developed, approved, and reviewed in conjunction with the HR Manager and other management as appropriate.

Make it part of basic management philosophy to avoid "across-the-board" reductions. The risk is too great that you will impact good people and/or productive operations. Avoid pitfalls by taking some time to ascertain what really makes sense. When planning a reduction, also begin planning your post-reduction communication to the survivors.

Employment at Will Is Real

Not just another government obstacle, employment at will is real and must be taken seriously. Even detailed personnel manuals won't necessarily preclude problems. Again, it is not so much what you do, but *how* you do it, how you say it. How you say it may well become an implied contract in the eyes of a court. You must make every effort to ensure that, in all of your areas of people responsibility, there is clear, concise and continuing dialogue about the subject. Employment at will may be a fair concept when both parties, employer and employee, handle their dealings professionally and objectively, but that realistically is a utopian thought. There are some similarities between changes in the employment-at-will concept and the advent of equal opportunity legislation in the early 1960s. These laws (for example, Civil Rights Act of 1964, the Equal Pay Act) were enacted because so many organizations gave only lip service to concepts of equal opportunity for qualified people, and equal pay for equal work. No organization admitted to discrimination because of race or religion or to not paying men and women equally for the same jobs—but in the real world, it happened. Because employers have been typically lax about all personnel practices, and in particular their termination practices and procedures, the concept of employment at will is being diluted and will continue to erode. So, this is a situation in which the government and the courts will be the enforcers if organizations don't pay strict attention to how they treat employees from the time they hire to the time they may have to fire.

It is your responsibility to understand and conduct activities in keeping with employment-at-will concepts and the organization's policies and procedures.

The Firing Manager

The point was made earlier in the text that the possibility of firing should be considered when hiring. This bit of negative philosophy may be just the impetus needed to work at hiring better, which should lessen the probability of terminating. The responsibility to fire is an integral part of your job—that point has been made repeatedly; and again, you must learn all you can about the process so you can deal most effectively with it.

You also have a responsibility in conjunction with the human resources manager to do pretermination planning and preparation. This is *not* last-minute planning, that would almost guarantee that things would get messed up. Understand what your resources are and be prepared to utilize all of them to ensure humane and sensitive terminations.

Planning should cover at a minimum all the details outlined in the termination checklist. Planning will develop the selection criteria for who should go. Planning ensures direct and honest communication. Planning also considers post-termination concerns. This planning will be based on the values and goals believed in by all levels of management, in all functional areas of the organization. Planning is based on realistic policies and procedures administered with fairness and continuity. Procedures are essential for fair administration, because a policy vacuum in any phase of business will create a real liability for the organization, and in relation to terminations, it may be disastrous. Your responsibility as the firing manager, when it occurs, is to be aware of all the implications of terminating, with particular emphasis on the psychology (the total impact) of terminations. You must be aware that something is wrong, that the organization has had a failure, whether attributable to hiring, training, environment, poor management, et cetera. The objective of your business has not been met if people have to be let go.

Be the Great Communicator

Many of your managerial responsibilities in avoiding pitfalls have been discussed. Avoiding most of them will require you also to be a great communicator. The failure to communicate well causes most of the problems in business as well as in life in general. In *A Passion for Excellence,* Peters and Austin say, "The number one managerial problem in America is, quite simply, managers who are *out of touch with their people* and out of touch with their customers."[15] Employees look to management in troubled times (when there is a crisis), and when management doesn't respond, either through arrogance or complete isolation, people will be frightened and concerned.

John Brennan, author of *The Conscious Communicator,* said: "Communication is the glue that holds a society together. The ability to communicate enables people to form and maintain personal relationships. And the quality of such relationships depends on the caliber of communication between the parties."[16] He later noted, somewhat tongue-in-cheek, that in the Garden of Eden, "Adam got the word, but missed the message."[17] That may say it all about communication in many organizations.

Communication, to be effective, must be considered in light of a number of factors:

People usually act like they understand what is said, but really don't.

Don't expect understanding when communication in the organization is a "sometime" thing.

People, as a generalization, distrust management and will be very dubious of things not explained well, that is, that they don't understand. If managers "share the news," good or bad, people will believe in them and the organization.

Credibility is the key to an organization's communications, and the burden for developing credibility belongs to the manager. Credibility exists when policies, procedures, rules, etc., are understood.

The culture of an organization is heavily influenced by communication. A good culture encourages open communication.

Good communication promotes efficiency—it saves time by avoiding second-guessing and confusion.

Communication will be as good as are your employee relations—where individuals feel they are treated as individuals, they will be receptive.

Good communication helps people to feel part of the organization and they will have more concern for what happens.

If you don't provide accurate and timely information, it will be gotten from other sources, and will probably be distorted or inaccurate.

Too many managers and organizations condone a communications philosophy that is harmful and disruptive. This approach is what the author refers to as crisis communication: when things are bad, managers want to communicate to say, "everything will be fine if *we* do this and if *we* do that, if we all pull together now." This type of occasional communication won't make up for all the previous neglect. This is not to say that a crisis (such as a cutback in personnel) should *not* be communicated, but rather that it should not be the only time.

The organization or manager with self-inflicted wounds does not really understand that every employee is entitled to information—obviously not all the details of everything that's taking place in the organization, but certainly everything that can be public. Such an organization assumes "they won't know the difference, so we can tell them what we want." In that type of environment, employees can almost always differentiate between facts and garbage, and are usually already suspicious.

The point is made repeatedly about terminations that "bad news travels fast," and more often than not, it gets distorted. It's not just the employees— bad news travels fast outside of the organization, too. Rumors always seem to develop, and almost always exaggerate any story. The more direct and honest you and the organization can be, the better the chance that the news won't be confused.

When terminating is the subject, the fear of firing for the manager and organization is that they will come off as bad guys, and often, this causes them to become mute about communication of any kind. You are afraid that you will be blamed as the guy who made it happen—which is usually the truth. So, the usual approach is to play it close to the vest; the less said, the better. "It's our problem and our business, so we aren't obligated to tell anyone"—that's when you really get wounded.

The past few years are rife with stories about organizations that felt no obligation to communicate termination information to anyone. A large company in a southern state, prime employer in town and owner of the local television station, made a staff reduction of thirty-five people, but management was adamant that no one outside the organization be told. When the question of the media was raised, the response was, "We own the television station." The local news that evening "confirmed the report of the layoff of 435 people at XYZ today." The unwillingness to share the correct information proved the old adage that "rumors are always ten times worse than the truth." A retraction seldom gets the facts across, either; the damage is done.

Then there was the high-tech company, who in spite of a history of layoffs, now faced shutdown of an operation. The company attitude was: "We don't have to involve any outsiders in this process. It's our problem, we have faced it before." Even though *they* had been through it before, the employees had not, and the announcement on a Friday afternoon hit like a thunderbolt. Within thirty minutes of the announcement, the local television station was set up in the employee parking lot, interviewing affected employees. Not many kind words were exchanged, and the corporate office was in an uproar over the situation.

A wise organization and manager should learn something from past mistakes and build in the controls so it won't happen again. Are good communications important? Just remember, the problems involved in terminations are primarily communication problems.

Summary

To avoid pitfalls in terminations, you as a manager need to concentrate on three major points. First, probably the most frequent and worst mistake any manager makes is to procrastinate about a losing situation. Secondly, a major responsibility of management is to ensure that everyone knows where they stand at all times (immediately and for the foreseeable future). This does not mean making specific promises, but rather that any employee should know how they are being viewed, now and for the future. Failure to be open and honest is ineffective management, and unfair to the employee.

Third, you must have control. To be in control, there must be a system of standards (policies and procedures) for you to measure against, so that errors can be avoided or certainly detected and dealt with. Having control means taking action necessary to correct a situation, whatever form that action may take. To be in control means to have confidence that you are fulfilling all of your managerial responsibilities in the most professional and responsible manner. That's how to avoid the pitfalls.

6
The Human Resources Manager's Role: Control and Training

The real challenge that faces the human resources (HR) manager, and the reason that he or she must assume a more assertive role in terminations, relates to the changed work environment and employee attitudes of today. These two factors require a great deal more attention to interpersonal relationships. Interpersonal skills have become magnified by the "age of litigation." This is also a period when we will see fewer opportunities for people; loyalty will continue to erode; people will show less flexibility; and so on. Managing under these conditions is difficult, and more so when compounded by continuing pressures of restructuring, downsizing and reorganization. These pressures often mean the organization must do more with less—not less for the sake of less, but to increase efficiency.

Every organization strives to attain or retain competitive edge and that becomes more difficult every day. This means that the HR manager's role must be expanded to become more visible and involved. Recent studies and surveys of top management indicate the need for greater involvement. This new emphasis is due to the increasing recognition that people really are the organization's most important asset; it's no longer a management cliché. All people tasks are more complicated and expensive today, so they must be done right if the organization is to survive.

Terminating is more complicated and expensive, as are all of the other pieces in the linkage, like hiring. The HR manager therefore must expand his or her role in developing, disseminating and monitoring relevant policy. Also, there is a key role in training, training so that everyone understands "how" to deal with people. It isn't what you do to a person in terminating, but *how* you do it that has the real impact; the fact that you do appraisals is fine, but *"how"* is critical; *how* you bring people into the organization; *how* you orient new employees to the organization—all of these aspects contribute to an individual's success or failure.

Employment at Will—A New Ball Game

As noted in chapter 1, nearly 70 percent of the work force in the United States is employed without any written contract or agreement relative to their tenure on the job. Employment at will, a long-standing concept, allowed people to be terminated for most any reason. That's the way it was until fairly recently. Now, however with the concept being regularly challenged in the courts, it's a different environment that requires that your house be in order—in terms of both printed materials, and verbal commitments made knowingly or unknowingly to *potential* employees or employers.

So much concern exists about this phase of employee/employer relations because most nonunion employees are not covered by any specific procedures such as those spelled out in labor agreements. Thus, what is said to potential or existing employees and the organization's written materials (like the employee handbook) form the logical target for termination issues. Much of the litigation instituted by employees is by exempt employees—professional and managerial. As a rule, they may know more about their rights and the obligation of the employer. As noted earlier, the individual in a termination scenario usually suffers and loses more than the organization both financially and emotionally, and may react in what may appear to be an illogical manner.

People are increasingly aware that there are basically three exceptions to employment at will: public policy, implied contract, and good faith and fair dealing. Possibly the most sensitive area for the majority of organizations is the implied contract, because this can apply to any job candidate. It may be a verbal statement by personnel or the hiring manager, or after employment by either of these parties, as well as others in authority. It may be the written word in an employee handbook, on an employment application form, the company's personnel policy manual, the performance appraisal forms, etc., relative to continuity of employment. Moreover, the history of EEO litigation has resulted in a much greater awareness of "rights" by most people, and they will feel much freer to raise questions if they feel they have been mistreated. Promises should thus not be made about job security, permanent or lifetime employment, long-term training, opportunities for career advancement, or salary increases.

If we consider how many individuals have the opportunity to say or do something that could be considered "illegal," it is overwhelming. Everyone a job candidate meets during the recruiting, selection and placement process poses a potential danger of implied contractual obligations. There are also all of the figures of authority—immediate supervisor, and other, more senior people in the organization with whom they may deal. There must be a well-conceived plan for communicating the organization's policies, procedures and practices to minimize these risks. This is a real test for the HR manager: to develop the organizational awareness that will prevent employment at will violations.

Audit or Litigate

A first step for any organization in getting its house in better order is an audit of personnel practices. Fred Foulkes has stated: As discussed, personnel has three primary functions. The first function relates to the development of personnel policies. The second function relates to personnel's traditional advice and counsel and service role. The third function, one which seems to be *growing in importance, relates to personnel's auditing role.* Audits are a feedback mechanism undertaken to assure top management that the company's policies and practices are being carried out as they are supposed to be.[18] This could not be said better in the context of termination practices! Employment-at-will litigation is very difficult for employers, because the interpretation varies of what is "right" and "fair." Every organization should fine-tune its personnel practices to ensure they are effective and fault-free. The difficult part is that much of litigation may hinge on one person's word versus the word of another. An employee or potential employee will remember what was said to him or her, but an employer dealing with dozens or hundreds of people may well not remember.

Also, recruiting brochures and other company publications have historically portrayed an unrealistic situation—every organization promises a great future, has the best geographic living conditions, the best benefits, ad nauseam. Because employees do remember what was said to them, the danger of it being construed as an implied contract is high. Too many organizations make promises or suggest things to satisfy then-potential employees in order to recruit them. Tell them whatever they want to hear, but get them on the payroll!

The tendency to promise the world to get a "yes" from the prospective employee is very dangerous. The courts are fairly pragmatic: "You said something—you promised something."

When Susan Elmer of Glue-All, Inc. was recruiting Jack Schulte, there was a bit of an impasse on compensation. Jack indicated he could not accept the job with the offer Susan proposed, even though he was intensely interested in the job. Susan said they just could not budge on the numbers now. She suggested a solution—she would set up an earlier formal review date of eight months, rather than the usual twelve months. She also indicated that Jack could anticipate a substantial increase, which would more than make up the difference.

Jack came to work, and after seven months, it was obvious the situation was not working between him and his boss. Jack was terminated, and he was quite upset about the whole situation, not least about the compensation issue.

Jack initiated legal action, and the court was very sympathetic to Jack's argument that Glue-All said: "We can't pay you enough to start, but we will make you 'more than whole' in a specified period of time." Glue-All's implication was that Jack would be employed for a stipulated period of time, as stated by Susan.

Granted, Jack should have been smart enough to get things in writing, and Susan should have known that the promise was an implied contract.

However, the desire to sign Jack on overcame good judgment and commonsense.

The message is clear: don't make statements that you don't (or are not willing to) write down. If they are not "company-credible," they shouldn't be made, because they can't be put in writing anyway if they aren't approved. Most employment-at-will problems result from lack of commonsense and good business judgment!

Many organizations still tend to sell more than they can produce relative to people's careers. This is a particular trap in relation to the employment process, where many things get said in the heat of the battle—when the level of interest in acquiring the individual rises and the sales pitch starts. Another trap is found in statements printed in employment brochures or other company literature that imply binding agreements or promises of some kind. These things can come home to haunt, as more courts and juries are proving.

Kara Lee was terminated from her job after two years as a marketing analyst at Klose, Inc. for failing to complete a project on the scheduled date. It was completed two days later, but Kara's boss told her that she wasn't performing well and had to go.

Kara was appalled because she had consistently good performance reviews during her tenure at Klose. Her husband was equally upset when she told him, and suggested she contact an attorney, which she did the following day. The attorney reviewed, in detail, Kara's career with Klose, including her recollection of the details of the selection process she was exposed to, and a review of pertinent company policies and publications. It became apparent that Kara had been told by both the personnel department and the hiring manager that she would have a real future at Klose, Inc. with her education, experience and motivation, and would move rapidly up the marketing ladder if she performed as they were sure she could. The company's career brochure also stated that "with adequate performance, every employee has a bright future at Klose."

The case eventually went to court, and the personnel department's remarks, along with the hiring manager's, the brochure's statement about performance, and Kara's consistently good performance reviews persuaded the jury that she was performing her job above the standards set, even though this particular project was late. It cost Klose, Inc. court costs, back pay, and the chagrin of having to reinstate Kara.

A primary objective of conducting an audit of your employment and other personnel practices is to minimize the organization's potential vulnerability. It is also a good opportunity to examine the efficiency and effectiveness of your people practices. This involves asking some hard questions and seeking honest and objective information to reduce the possibility of unlawful and inconsistent personnel policies, practices and procedures. The organization's human resources department should conduct this review. In a sense, this should really be an ongoing process, to be certain that the practicing managers are constantly reminded of their role in not compromising the organization by suggesting things that may be unrealistic or construed as an implied contract.

There is controversy as to whether employee handbooks and personnel policies constitute an employment contract. A number of significant court decisions have ruled them to be contractual documents. Some excellent guidelines in auditing handbooks and policies are taken from the *Employment Law Bulletin* of the Boston law firm of Gaston Snow & Ely Barlett:

> Issues to bear in mind when providing employee handbooks to non-union employees include:
>
> - Signing for handbook. By requiring an employee to sign for the handbook or agree to its terms, an employer may be perceived by courts to be treating the handbook as a contract.
> - Disclaimer. Several courts—including those in Michigan and New Jersey—have indicated that language disclaiming the legal enforceability of a handbook will be effective. Such disclaimer should be clear and should appear at the beginning of the handbook.
> - Reservation of right to amend. Courts have been less willing to enforce handbooks as contracts where the employer reserved the right to amend the handbook at any time and at its own discretion.
> - Fair treatment. It is dangerous to use the handbook as a public relations vehicle for employees. The gratuitous statement that it is the company's policy to treat employees "fairly" will only result in fairness becoming an issue to be decided by the court or jury. What is "fair" will no longer be determined by the employer. Similar references to just or good cause for discipline or termination should be avoided.
> - Permanent/probationary employees. Several courts have considered the issue of whether "permanent" employees are just that, and therefore may only be terminated for good cause. Since probationary period is simply an early review period, it should be treated as such. The term "permanent" employee should be avoided.
> - Progressive discipline. While a system of progressive discipline is often advisable, overly complicated procedures—including those with various steps and timetables—can be cumbersome and prone to error. An employee who has not been disciplined in strict conformity with handbook policies may file suit claiming breach of contract.
> - Conformity of personnel documents. Employee handbooks, application forms, and offer letters should be consistent; each should reference the employer's at-will employment policy, disclaim guaranteed employment, and avoid language that might suggest the documents constitute a binding contract.[19]

A reasonable approach to this type of audit is to "see how you are doing." To be realistic, although it may sound like a negative approach, have people begin to think about terminations when they hire new employees. If you have to think it might not work, you will pay more attention to proper procedures in dealing with them. The hiring procedure in many organizations is so often where the problems start—not only from the employment-at-will perspective, but also from the standpoint of the "wrong hire" (the person terminated six months after starting because he/she just wasn't "right.")

The failure of an individual employee is costly to the employee, as well as to the organization, so it behooves any organization to minimize the failure risk by ensuring that its managers understand their role in the employment obligation. Managers also need to realize that one of their major responsibilities is hiring the right people. They should be party to this audit, reviewing policy and procedures, because poor employment practices can allow the wrong person to be hired.

Poor employment practices generally exist where there are few or no controls on manpower. There must be controls if an organization hopes for any success in today's competitive labor market. The manpower process must be given the same thought and attention as any other aspect of the business. It is a matter for the decision-makers, the management of the organization. The HR manager should be facilitator and umpire in ensuring conformity to policy and procedure. Poor employment practices often exist because there is no real definition, and without that, it is hard to assign responsibility.

Gaining Control

Organizations are in control when they have established their style of management and their culture. Policy has a great deal to do with this—it sets the stage. Because of the negative and potentially litigious nature of terminations, strict controls have to be established. Standards for measuring performance have to be set so that errors can be detected early and action taken to correct them.

It is increasingly apparent, then, that an organization's effectiveness requires specific policies, procedures, and excellent internal communications about all its personnel dealings, or it may be in front of a judge. Simply trusting individual judgment in people dealings won't work; there are too many pitfalls, and there must be written guidelines. Because organizations have lost much latitude in terminating employees through continued challenges to the employment-at-will concept, a great deal of effort must be made to alleviate the problem. Juries have little sympathy for organizations, particularly big ones. An organization can't "just fire someone" anymore; it has become much more complex than that.

Personnel policies should never be developed in a crisis atmosphere. They require time and thought to make them part of the organization's strategy. Nor should they be developed by any one entity—too many aspects need to be considered (legal, ethical, needs of employees, cost, etc.). Policies must always be developed with the goals and values of the organization in mind.

The HR manager's major input on these termination-related policies will be to offer perspective on what is being done elsewhere, what significant social changes need to be considered, and what is realistic vis-à-vis the organization and its culture." Practicing and HR managers must jointly make judgments about policy from three perspectives: Are they understandable and easily implemented? Will they work effectively in the manner for which they are intended? Will they make a positive contribution to the goals of the organization?

The guiding philosophy in developing or revising pertinent policies and procedures on recruitment, development and termination of people should be always to endeavor to treat people on an honest and equitable basis. Policies additionally should ensure maximum input from the practicing manager before anything is adopted. There are many considerations in developing any policy; for example, what's the expected profit impact? Policies and procedures must then be administered with due regard for all the ethical, legal and economic considerations of doing business in today's highly complex and mobile society.

What Are Policies?

What, then, is a policy, and what is a procedure within the context of today's confusing business world? Policy in reality is a strategy, a principle, or rule. It should define the subject's role in the overall philosophy of the organization. Effective policy must be:

an expression of belief or intent—the underlying principles governing what the organization does or hopes to do in the subject area;

stated in broad terms;

long-range;

developed through active participation of practicing managers;

approved by organization's highest authority;

inviolate; and

expressed in writing.

The fifth point may be the critical one, inasmuch as without top management's support and approval, any policy will in all likelihood be ineffective. It must be management's responsibility to ensure it is understood and accepted by the organization. Managers must be an active voice in the process, and then human resources can be the implementer and monitor.

Policies set the parameters for operating the organization. Policies are the plan for getting the job done. Policies provide the framework for procedures in the organization. Procedures are the instructions for getting the job done—a guide for the day-to-day operations. Procedures evolve and are developed from policy, at the operating levels of the organization.

Policy statements can be simple or complex. Each organization may take a different approach to the specific subject matter of a given policy. In formulating a termination policy, the organization's own conscience, its location, the types of jobs, all may influence what will be done for people leaving. The important thing is that a policy statement reflect the philosophy of the organization relative to each phase of the subject. Again, in a termination policy, retirement, resignation, discharge, layoff must all be covered.

The most important, "must-have" policy statements in the context of terminations are the following. These are the basic policies needed to provide control on the linkage of termination:

employment policy (how to acquire people)

termination policy, and policy on termination of employment due to performance (how to let people go)

separation pay policy (involuntary termination pay rules)

exit interview policy (the mechanics of leaving)

outplacement policy (job-hunting assistance to be provided)

It would be extremely difficult, if not impossible, to spell out *one* definitive policy statement on any of these subjects that would be applicable to all organizations. Just as every organization is unique, so each policy will be unique to the organization. To be effective, however, policy must be practical and real-world–oriented, and attuned to getting the job done in the particular environment of the organization. The sample policies are a compilation of the thinking of a number of different organizations in diverse industries on a particular subject. It is hoped that they will provide a point of departure in developing, reviewing or revising policy statements.

There is one final and very critical point to bear in mind in developing or reviewing your policies and procedures. A statement should be included in both your employee handbook and your policy manual that is similar to the following:

> None of the information in this handbook/manual should be construed as a contract of employment. Any employee is free to terminate employment voluntarily with proper notice, and the XYZ Corporation may terminate an employee at any time for any reason. Any statements or promises, written or oral, to the contrary are hereby expressly disavowed and should not be relied upon by a prospective employee or an existing employee of XYZ Corporation. Additionally, the contents of this handbook/manual are subject to change at the discretion of XYZ Corporation at any time.

Even though organizations may change the contents of a policy at any time, there is still a good deal of confusion about what will stand up legally—the old, existing policy or the new policy. So, discretion is still the better part of valor—pay strict attention to all your dealings with employees, and plan to train, train, train!

Sample Policies

Employment Policy

Policy. The policy of the XYZ Corporation with respect to employment is to use every reasonable means available to select the best candidate for the position to be filled in order to achieve our objectives of profit and growth. It is corporate policy to fill position vacancies by promotion from within. When this is not possible, we will recruit externally. Our employment procedures and practices shall be in compliance with all local, state, and federal laws. (There will be fair and equal employment opportunity for all, with no discrimination because of race, color, age, sex, creed, or national origin.) Recruiting activities will be conducted with due regard for our relationships with customers, competitors, suppliers, and other companies.

Responsibilities.

1. Completion of Personnel Requisition Form #88A is a joint responsibility of the Human Resources (HR) Department and the line department with the vacancy. The HR Department is responsible for obtaining the necessary approvals.
2. The selection of sources to be utilized will be the responsibility of the HR Department. Line departments will communicate any source contact

to the HR Department to ensure maximum efficiency and economy in their use.

3. The HR Department will be responsible for scheduling interviews with all candidates.

   a. All candidates should have a minimum of two interviews (one with HR and one with the appropriate department).

   b. Candidates for more senior positions will have enough interviews to ensure the best exposure for both them and the Corporation.

4. The HR Department will be responsible for ensuring compliance with corporate policy on equal employment opportunity (EEO) and for ensuring an understanding of employment at will.

   a. HR will inform all solicited sources of corporate EEO policy and of their expected compliance.

   b. HR will communicate information about EEO laws, executive orders, employment at will, etc., to all organization components.

5. References are the responsibility of the HR Department and should usually be done by the person who conducted the interview. In certain instances, the line department interviewer should assist in checking references, particularly when an unusual or highly technical job is involved.

6. The HR Department is responsible for coordinating the pre-employment physical examination with the Medical Department or with an outside physician. The Medical Department is responsible for interpreting results of the exam and notifying the HR Department.

7. The HR Department will be responsible for compiling and discussing all selection information with the hiring manager to arrive at the hire/not hire decision.

8. The HR Department is responsible for extending offers of employment and for preparing the offer letter. All job offers will be approved by the appropriate line manager, with concurrence by the HR Department. Disagreement on the dollar offer or other details will be resolved by the vice-president of HR.

9. The HR Department is responsible for organizing and coordinating the "formal" orientation program for new employees. The line department is responsible for orienting the new employee to his/her specific responsibilities and to the departmental organization.

Procedures

1. The existence of a budgeted or replacement vacancy or a request for an addition to the head count in any department must be approved prior to initiating any recruitment activity. Personnel Requisition Form #88A specifies the necessary approvals.

2. The HR Department must have the approved Personnel Requisition Form #88A to recruit potential employees effectively and ensure:
   a. compliance with the budget.
   b. compliance with established salary ranges.
   c. understanding of the requirements and responsibilities of the position.
3. The HR Department has full discretionary power to recruit (by best available means) and to recommend candidates for potential employment.
4. Initial interviews will be conducted by the HR department, with subsequent interviews (as necessary) conducted by the line Departments.
5. All candidates will be required to complete and sign the Application for Employment Form #99.
6. All recruitment activities will be conducted in compliance with the corporation's policy of equal employment opportunity.
7. Reference checks will be conducted on all candidates of interest. This will be done to confirm interview results, as well as to elicit further information. Offers will not be extended until satisfactory information has been obtained. In unusual circumstances, offers may be extended contingent on satisfactory reference. All reference activity will be conducted with due regard for the procedures required by the Fair Credit Reporting Act, Public Law 91-508.
8. All offers will be contingent on the candidate's passing a pre-employment physical examination successfully. Potential employees not recommended for hire by the examining physician will not be extended offers. Exceptions to this must be approved by the vice-president of HR.
9. The HR Department and the hiring department will develop the offer, taking into consideration salary policy and the candidate's current salary, experience, potential, etc.
   a. Offers should be extended verbally if possible and followed up by a letter specifying details. Salary will always be expressed in monthly terms.
   b. All offers should contain a statement to the effect that "this offer constitutes the total agreement and supersedes any prior statements or agreements." See Exhibit A.
10. Expenses involved in the employment process, with the exception of relocation expenses, will be charged to HR Account #EE-6.
11. Each new employee will be required to attend an orientation program.
    a. The new employee will complete all required and necessary forms, for example, W-2 form, group insurance, patent and inventions agreements, etc.
    b. This program is to acquaint the new employee with the Corporation and its policies.

Exhibit A

PERSONAL & CONFIDENTIAL

Date

Dear _____:

This letter will confirm the terms of our offer of employment for the position of Assistant Controller at XYZ Corporation, reporting to Richard Breen.

We are pleased to offer you this position at a salary of $6,000 per month. As we discussed with you, this position makes you eligible for incentive income (bonus). Inasmuch as you will not be an employee for the full year, your bonus for this year will be prorated from the time you report to work.

This offer is contingent upon your satisfactory completion of a pre-employment medical examination, which we can arrange for you. Or, you may go to your personal physician. If you choose the latter course, have your physician forward the results and his bill to Dr. Franks, our medical director, at this address.

Listed below are the benefits coverage applicable to you.

1. *Insurance*

   You will be eligible for $00000 term life insurance, which carries over if you should retire in the amount of $00000. This insurance is paid for by the company. There is no waiting period involved to become eligible for this insurance coverage, which also includes *normal hospitalization*. *Major medical* is a contributory group program, and you may enroll with no waiting period. This is a premium of $000 per month. Your *long-term disability* coverage will cost you $00 per month. The amount of benefits payable under this plan is $0000 per month. In addition, you will be covered by an *accidental death and dismemberment* policy in the amount of $0000 and a *business-travel accident policy* in the amount of $0000. Both of these are noncontributory plans.

2. *Retirement*

   The Retirement Income Plan is a noncontributory final pay-type plan. You would be eligible to participate after two years of service, and if you retire from Acme you would receive payments as outlined in your Employee Benefits booklet.

3. *Stock Option*

   This position entitles you to stock option, subject to approval by a committee of the Board of Directors. This will be recommended to the committee as soon as possible after you report to work. The initial offering will be for *x* shares. Option price is based on 100 percent of market price on date of grant.

4. *Vacation*
   You are eligible for X weeks vacation, based on a length-of-service formula.

5. You will receive a comprehensive annual physical examination each year you are employed. This is voluntary and at no cost to you.

6. We are scheduled on a 40-hour week. The work day is from 8 A.M. to 5 P.M., with an hour for lunch.

7. We are paid bimonthly, on the 15th and 30th.

8. As discussed, we will pay the cost of your relocation from Chicago to the greater New York area, within the guidelines spelled out in the enclosed procedure.

This offer constitutes the total agreement and supersedes any prior statements or agreements.

We are pleased that you will be visiting the weekend of July 7–8, and should you have any problems or questions, please call me at work, (212) 719-8474, or at home, (201) 377-2121.

Further details of the various benefits programs are outlined in the enclosed booklet. If you have any questions about these or any other aspect of your employment, we will be glad to clarify them for you. Needless to say, all of us who have been involved in discussions with you are extremely anxious for you to join us and are looking forward to it.

Very truly yours,

cc: Jones Assoc.
     C.R. Bryan (Corporate Finance Dept.)

Performance Appraisal Program Policy

Policy. The Corporate Performance Appraisal Program (CPAP) has been established to provide three critical end products to the Corporation: (1) To administer candid, meaningful performance appraisals and successfully to implement agreed-upon career plans, in order to maximize utilization of all employees. (2) To ensure that an employee's performance objectives/work plans support key business objectives and priorities. (3) To provide better data for human resource planning/decision making.

Objectives. Management has initiated several major developments to improve the stewardship of its human resources and provide the environment for employee self-development. These developments will be characterized by our CPAP, which has been developed to increase candor and openness in the supervisor-employee dialogue about performance and career planning; increase employee knowledge about performance measurements and career assessment; ensure a formal career and performance appraisal program that will further develop managers' appraisal and counseling skills; ensure that managers are the key professional resources for their employees and will fulfill their responsibilities for development of their subordinates.

Responsibilities

1. Each professional employee will establish clear, concise, measurable and meaningful objectives/work plans for his or her position in the organization. This objective-setting part of CPAP exists to:

    a. Provide a better understanding of work expectations

    b. Utilize the supervisor-subordinate dialogue for developing high input strategies for achieving performance results

    c. Improve employee performance through continual monitoring, shaping and prioritizing of objectives/work plans.

2. Each manager, as part of his/her total management responsibility, is accountable for the development of his/her human resources. In CPAP, this accountability encompasses three specific responsibilities:

    a. Establishing with each subordinate a written set of performance objectives that reflect current/future business needs, and updating these objectives as needed;

    b. Reviewing these objectives as a part of a total performance review, and discussing with each subordinate career planning;

    c. Completing performance reviews and career-planning discussions by the end of the fourth quarter.

General

1. CPAP involves each professional employee in the performance appraisal process through:

    a. Self-appraisal as a part of the regular review;

    b. A performance appraisal review that includes discussion of performance/career planning;

    c. Acknowledgment of the review by signing a completed appraisal form.

2. CPAP invites and encourages each employee to develop his/her own

career plans with guidance and informed assistance from a supervisor. The career-planning part of CPAP requires that each employee be responsible for his/her own career planning, and stresses the importance of the supervisor's review and realistic assessment of these career/interests and establishes a mutually agreed upon plan for achievement.

3. Each manager's successful accomplishment of his or her responsibilities will result in balanced feedback to a subordinate about individual strengths and shortcomings. This information can then be used to make more informed decisions about improving job performance and developing career plans. It will also ensure:

    a. That an employee's performance objectives/work plans support key business objectives and priorities;

    b. The development of realistic plans for improving each employee's job performance;

    c. Increased trust and communication between manager and subordinates;

    d. Frequent balanced feedback about performance.

    e. Effective utilization of information from this process will provide the basis for total human resource planning in the Corporation.

Termination Policy

Policy. The employment relationship may be terminated at any time by the employee or the Corporation. It is the Corporation's policy to handle all terminations of employment in as dignified and equitable a manner as possible. The Corporation's policy prohibits any contracts of employment unless they are in writing and have the written approval of the president and CEO and the vice-president, Human Relations. No other employee or representative of the Corporation has the authority to enter into any agreement for employment for a specified period of time, or to make any agreement contrary to this policy.

Guidelines

1. *Company-Initiated Terminations*
    Discharge is initiated by management for violation of organization policy or rules, unsatisfactory performance, or other disciplinary reasons. *Layoff* is initiated by management for purposes of reorganization of a work area, because of lack of work, cost reduction efforts, or other operational reasons.

a. In all Company-initiated terminations, it is necessary to have appropriate documentation detailing the rationale (for example, cost reduction, reorganization) or undesirable and/or unacceptable work or behavior that supports the Company's position.

b. Before an employee may be terminated, approval must be obtained from at least two higher levels of the employee's management, *as well as* the appropriate Human Resources representative.

c. The Law Department must review any termination where the employee is covered by EEO laws. This includes any employee who is a minority, female, or forty or more years of age. It is the responsibility of Human Resources to present the facts regarding the potential termination to the Law Department.

d. The termination of an employee with ten years or more of service must be approved by the vice-president of personnel and the president. It is the responsibility of Human Resources to provide the president with a written summary of the reasons for the termination.

2. *Employee-Initiated Terminations*
   Resignation is initiated at the request of the employee through written notification indicating the reason(s) for leaving and the intended last day of work. *Retirement* is initiated by the employee through written notification indicating intent to retire and the intended last day of work.

   a. Any employee who wishes to resign will be at liberty to do so without prejudice. The Corporation requires a minimum of two weeks' notice so that arrangements for a replacement can be made.

   b. The employee's supervisor should submit a termination notice to the appropriate Human Resources representative so that preparations for an orderly termination can be initiated.

   c. Where appropriate, the supervisor will remind the terminating employee of his or her obligations as listed the Employee Confidential Information Agreement, and will ask him or her to sign the agreement.

3. *Exit Interviews*

   a. After the termination notice has been received by the Human Resources Department, arrangements will be made to have the employee participate in an exit interview conducted by the appropriate Human Resources representative.

   b. If there is no Human Resources representative available, (for example, as in Field Sales terminations), the exit interview will be conducted by the management person responsible for the supervision of the terminating employee.

c. If an exit interview cannot be conducted, a letter requesting the customary exit interview information will be sent to the employee by the Human Resources Department.

4. *Severance Pay Considerations*

a. In certain situations, severance pay must be awarded to the terminating employee. To qualify, the employee must meet the following conditions:

(1) Must have completed one year of service.

(2) The termination must not in the judgment of the Corporation have been for cause, including, but not limited to, incidents outlined in the "Disciplinary Action" policy under "Termination."

(3) The termination must have been initiated by the Corporation. Employees who resign voluntarily are not eligible for severance pay.

b. Severance pay is based on age and length of service (with a minimum of one week, regardless) and will be disbursed to any qualified terminating employees as follows:

Severance Pay Schedule

Age	Amount of Severance Pay
Less than 30	1 week's pay per year of service
30–39	1½ weeks' pay per year of service
40–49	2 weeks' pay per year of service
50 +	2½ weeks' pay per year of service

c. An aggregate severance payment which would exceed $75,000 must have the prior approval of the vice-president for Human Resources of the Corporation.

d. Exception to the above schedule must be approved by the appropriate director of Human Resources.

5. *Outplacement Services*

a. Outplacement counseling may be offered on an individual basis as requested, upon approval by the Human Resources Department.

b. Employees who are offered *and accept* counseling may be provided support services at the discretion of the Corporation.

    c. Expenses for outplacement services will be paid for by the terminating department.

Termination of Employment Due to Performance

The Corporation sets and requires high standards of performance and conduct for all its employees. Members of management and supervision will ensure fair and consistent treatment for all employees.

    It is expected that supervisors will devote appropriate effort to retain competent employees who can make a good contribution to the organization. This includes taking corrective measures where necessary to help the employee understand and carry out his/her work responsibilities. All employees are to be given a reasonable opportunity to demonstrate value to the Corporation, including possible usefulness elsewhere within the organization. Involuntary termination should only occur as a proper last resort. Should such terminations occur, appropriate counseling and outplacement service will be made available to the terminated person.

    Note: In the event of any action by an employee resulting in discharge or termination for cause, the requirement for corrective measure to improve performance is waived. Any such terminations will still require, however, the review as outlined in Procedures 3 and 4. Also, the following Policy and Procedure is not intended to replace or override any written company/location policy covering "Probationary Employees," which may include "shorter" time periods for demonstrating satisfactory performance.

Policy. Should employee performance be less than satisfactory and, after proper counseling and a reasonable period of time, established objectives, standards, and/or job requirements are not met, the employee should be terminated. Separation pay for employees terminated under this Policy will be administered in accordance with the Separation Pay Policy. Exit interviews will be held with all employees leaving the organization, and outplacement service will be offered as appropriate.

Procedure

1. Where performance measured against previously determined work objectives is less than good, corrective measures should be taken. Counseling to review performance shortcomings, culminating in a general plan of improvement for the employee, should be held. To make sure there is no misunderstanding of the problem or the plan for improvement, this interview should be based on the corrective action to be taken and the Corporation's commitment to assisting the employee in meeting the action plan objectives.

2. If, after an appropriate time period (usually not longer than three months) required performance levels have not been attained, the employee should again be counseled with the action documented as outlined in 1 above. (The Performance Appraisal Review form may be used to document this action.) Emphasis should be focused on areas needing immediate improvement, the action plan to accomplish this purpose, including the employee's usefulness elsewhere where appropriate, and the consequence if improvement is not forthcoming. Higher supervisory levels and Human Resources should be involved at this stage.

3. If, after counseling and reasonable efforts by supervision and/or related staff professionals, performance is still not acceptable, the employee may be terminated. Responsibility for such action is the same as for the annual performance review, plus one level higher management of both line and Human Resource departments.

4. In all cases where the employee is salary level 15 or above, or is an exempt employee with ten or more years of service with the Corporation, the proposed termination must be reviewed and approved by the company president or corporate staff officer involved. Such individuals will be responsible for keeping the vice-president of Human Resources informed.

5. In instances where satisfactory improvement is made, the corrective interview forms maintained in the individual's file should be summarized as part of the employee's normal Performance Appraisal Review along with the current improved performance.

6. Employees terminated under this policy shall be processed in accordance with the provisions of the Separation Pay for Salaried Employees.

Separation Pay Policy for Salaried Employees

Policy. It is the policy of Super Corporation to provide separation pay to eligible employees resulting from certain types of involuntary terminations of employment for the purpose of providing a source of income during a period following termination and while other employment is being sought. Employees who voluntarily terminate shall not receive separation pay. The following sets forth the conditions under which this policy will be applied.

1. *Eligibility*
   a. All regular full-time employees of the Corporation with one or more years of continuous service, since their most recent date of hire, who are involuntarily terminated from active employment due to lack of work, shutdown of facilities, sale of all or part of a business (where the acquiring or purchasing company does not offer continued em-

ployment), or inability (except for physical and/or mental disability) to perform required duties may be considered for separation pay.

b. Employees who are terminated by reason of death, disability, retirement, discharge for cause, sale of all or part of a business (where the acquiring or purchasing company offers continued employment), failure to return to work following furlough or leave of absence, or for any other reason not specified in A above shall not be considered eligible for separation pay.

c. If an employee is involuntarily terminated due to the elimination of his/her job and elects to retire on account of the termination, separation pay up to a maximum of twenty-six weeks may be paid if approved by the vice-president, Employee Relations. All such requests are to be submitted by the Operating Company Personnel Director/Vice President.

2. *Separation Pay*

a. Separation pay shall be computed on the basis of one week for each full year of continuous service, plus one (1) additional week. For example, the following schedule indicates the allowance through five years of service.

Less than 1 year	0 weeks
1 year up to but not including 2 years	2 weeks
2 years up to but not including 3 years	3 weeks
3 years up to but not including 4 years	4 weeks
4 years up to but not including 5 years	5 weeks
5 years up to but not including 6 years	6 weeks

b. Except as provided in g (below), earnings from the time of notification of termination to actual termination should not be deducted from the separation pay.

c. Separation pay will be based upon the employee's base monthly salary, which shall not include overtime, shift premiums or any other premium payments.

d. Continuous service as defined in Administrative Procedure 4–1 shall be determined as of the employee's last day worked.

e. The separation pay specified above is independent of any vacation pay which may be payable under the Vacation Policy for Salaried Employees.

f. If an employee eligible to receive separation pay under this policy owes money to the Company at the time of termination, the Company, at its discretion, may deduct part of all of the amount owed from the separation pay.

g. In instances where an employee is being terminated due to inability to perform required duties and it is considered desirable to notify the employee of the termination in advance of the last day of work, the pay for any period of such notice in excess of two weeks shall be deducted from the separation pay.

3. *Unemployment Compensation*

a. State unemployment compensation has the same purpose as this policy, that is, to provide a source of income until an individual can find other employment.

b. It is the Company's intent that, where state law permits, an individual not receive both state unemployment compensation and separation pay for the same period of time. Even though separation pay is normally paid in a lump sum, it is pay for a specified number of weeks following termination. Therefore, all reports to the State Unemployment Compensation Board will clearly indicate that separation pay is being made and the number of weeks' pay the amount represents.

4. *Procedure*

a. Request for separation pay for a terminating employee should be processed on Form SC-1210 with the number of weeks' separation pay shown in the appropriate block. The SC-1210 should then be processed through normal channels and approval obtained in accordance with the salary level schedule contained in the Salary Administration Manual.

b. Requests for exception to this policy must be approved by the vice-president, Employee Relations.

c. Separation pay provided herein will be considered to include any termination notice or allowance which may be provided under an existing employment contract and will not be in addition to such notice or allowance. In those instances where the provisions of this policy exceed the contract requirements, the policy will apply.

5. *Submission of Claims and Claims Appeal*

a. If an employee feels the amount of payment is not correct (or if no payment is made within sixty days of the initial request for payment), he/she may file a written claim with Super Corporation for the unpaid amount.

b. In a written claim, an employee should specify the amount of his/her claim and any other data or information that he/she feels is pertinent. The written claim should be sent to Super Corporation, either direct (attention Corporate Employee Benefits, P.O. Box 324, Oshkosh, ID 20012), or through the local Personnel Department.

c. Within sixty days after receipt of claim by Super, the employee will be notified in writing of any denial of the claim. (If notice is not received within the 60-day period, the employee may regard the claim as denied). A notice of denial will include;

1. the specific reason(s) for denial;

2. specific reference to pertinent plan provisions on which the denial is based;

3. description of any additional material or information necessary to perfect the claim; and, an explanation of the plan's appeal procedure.

d. Within sixty days after notice of denial of a claim, an employee (or the employee's duly authorized representative) may file with the Super Corporation a written request for a review of the denial of the claim. Any denial upon review by the Corporation shall be made in writing, and shall include specific reasons for the denial (including reference to the pertinent Plan provisions on which the denial is based). Such decision shall be made no later than sixty days after Super's receipt of the request for review. Any action or determination by the Corporation in this review procedure shall be final, conclusive and binding upon the Company, its employees and every beneficiary.

6. *General*

a. The Separation Pay Policy is administered by Super Corporation, P.O. Box 324, Oshkosh, ID 20012, (712) 784-7840.

b. The Company pays the entire cost of the benefits under the Separation Pay Policy from its general assets.

c. Any records that are maintained under this policy will be maintained on a calendar-year basis.

d. The Corporation intends to continue the Separation Pay Policy indefinitely, but reserves the right to terminate or amend it.

Exit Interview Policy

Policy. The policy of the Corporation is to conduct exit (termination) interviews with all people leaving the organization. This policy provides basic guidelines (details may vary from division to division.) The exit interview will be conducted:

To determine reason(s) for leaving (if voluntary) and assess attitude and feeling toward organizations.

To ensure that details of employee benefits and final pay are explained.

To ensure that all documents, plans, drawings, etc., relative to the affairs of the corporation are returned.

To ensure understanding of continued obligations, with specific reference to Confidential/Proprietary Information and Inventions Agreement.

Procedure. Upon notification of employee's termination, the following procedure will be initiated.

1. The Immediate supervisor will ensure that employee turns in all company equipment and written materials, such as keys, tools or office equipment, uniforms, company manuals, all documents, plans, drawings or papers in any way relating to the affairs of the company, or any subsidiary or affiliated corporation, which may be in his or her possession or under his or her control. Supervisor will indicate completion by signing Employee Termination Clearance.

2. Human Resources Department

   a. Will conduct an exit interview with particular emphasis on:

      (1) reason(s) for leaving (if another job has been accepted, what are details).

      (2) overall assessment of type of work, advancement opportunity, compensation, benefits, working conditions, etc.

      (3) overall suggestions for improvement.

   b. Will ensure that employee benefits are discussed and necessary forms completed, i.e. conversion of life and medical insurance, savings plan payout, status under retirement income plan, continuation of basic medical insurance (if applicable), etc.

c. Will prepare a Termination Form #1422 and notify Payroll Department.

d. Will ensure that company property such as ID card or badge, and travel and telephone credit cards are turned in and will so indicate by signing Employee Termination Clearance Form. (Exhibit 3)

e. Will ensure that cash advances, home equity loan, etc., are settled satisfactorily. Where there is an outstanding supplemental relocation loan, that loan must be paid off by the last day of employment. If this is not possible, as determined by the location Human Resources Department, a written arrangement must be made for repayment within one year from the date of termination. The location Human Resources Department is responsible for the follow-up and control of such repayment arrangements, including advice and counsel from the Law Department if necessary.

f. In light of the increasing sensitivity of the various steps of the termination process, it is necessary to ensure continuity of contact with separating employees. Therefore, the designated individual in the Human Resources Department handling the exit procedure will distribute final paycheck to said employee.

3. If the individual *has accepted* another position:

a. Determine the planned duties of the individual in the new job without compromising any proprietary information. All individuals who may possess company secret or proprietary information must be informed of their continued obligations and their responsibility not to compromise it.

b. At the discretion of the company president a letter may be sent to the individual's new employer reemphasizing the obligations the person has. Copies of these letters will be furnished to the individual. (Such letters must be cleared by the Corporate Human Resources and Law departments in advance).

4. *All* individuals terminating employment will be apprised of their continuing obligation, and will be provided a copy of their signed Form #2716. The original form will be retained in the individual's personnel file as specified in Administrative Policy #10.

5. This section covers only termination of employment from active service either voluntarily or at company request. It does not cover employees who are terminated by reason of death, retirement, or following a period of leave of absence or disability.

   Upon termination of employment from active service, participation in and coverage under all benefits programs (group insurance, savings plan, retired income plan) ceases immediately.

   Terminating employees may have certain rights or options to exercise as outlined below. In all cases, the administration manual for the benefit program must be reviewed to determine these rights and/or options and these must be communicated to the employee.

   a. Group Insurance. Under most circumstances the basic hospital/surgical and the life insurance may be converted to an individual policy, and the employee will have a 31-day period following termination in which to make the conversion. The Group Insurance Administration Manual outlines the applicability of the conversion right and the procedure and forms that apply.

   b. Retired Income Plans. The Corporate Employee Benefits Department must be notified of the termination of all retirement plan participants. The Retired Income Plan Administrative Manual outlines the procedure and forms that apply. If the individual had participated in a contributory plan, a refund of contributions may be available. Those who have met the vesting requirements will receive a letter from the Corporate Employee Benefits Department outlining their rights.
   NOTE: A terminating employee aged fifty-five or older, but who is not vested, may nevertheless be eligible to request early retirement *prior* to termination. In such cases, unless the request is made *prior* to termination, all pension benefits will be canceled. The Retired Income Plan Administrative Manual outlines the procedure and forms that apply.

   c. Savings Plan. Participants will be entitled to a distribution and may be entitled to request a different form or different time of distribution. The Corporate Employee Benefits Department must be notified of the termination of all savings plan participants. The Savings Plan Administrative Manual outlines the procedure and forms that apply.

Exhibit 3

EMPLOYEE TERMINATION CLEARANCE FORM

Employee Name				Title	

Emp. #	Dept. #	Last Day Worked	Today's Date	Check to be Delivered to Supervisor	Mailed to Employee

Review the following items with the employee to determine that no company property is outstanding. Check items returned.

___ Keys to: Office/Files/Desk
___ Identification Card & Badge
___ Security Clearance
___ Company Manuals
___ Sales Incentive Plan
___ Marketing Sales Policy Manual
___ Sales Reference Handbook
___ Compensation Manual
___ Others
___ Library Books or Publications
___ Auto Insurance (Company Paid)
___ Cash Advances/Revolving Fund
   Amt. $___

___ Last Expense Report ___
   Amt. $___
___ Outstanding Expense Reports
___ Traveletters & Authorization
___ Credit Cards; Air/Tel./Etc.
___ Temporary Home Loan
___ Classified Materials
___ Other Company Equip. or Property
___ Stock Option Refund Due
___ Bond Deduction Refund Due
___ Credit Union Withdrawal Slip Attached

Discrepancies or Material Outstanding:

Vacation Entitlement Due: _____ Days
Present Year: _____ Days   Previous Year: _____

_____
Employee Signature

_____
Personnel Dept. Signature

Outplacement Policy

Policy. It is the intent of XYZ Corporation to provide a work environment which affords all employees the opportunity to demonstrate their value to the Corporation. However, XYZ Corporation can terminate the employment and compensation of an employee at any time with or without cause or notice, as can an employee. When circumstances exist where the employee is leaving the organization due to performance below expectations, career goals or expectations that cannot be met, or a reduction in the work force, outplacement services may be made available as appropriate. The objectives of this approach are (1) to reduce the hardship on the employee by providing counseling and advice on job-hunting techniques and assisting in career planning as appropriate; (2) through effective use of outplacement services, to improve the effectiveness of the terminated individual's job-hunting efforts and thus effect a quicker transition to a new job or career; and (3) to provide a positive impact on employees who remain through concern for those individuals affected, as well as goodwill on the part of the individual affected by easing the transition to a new job.

Procedures

1. The Corporate Human Resources Department will be responsible for the administration and interpretation of this policy. Specifically, the department will:

    a. Provide day-to-day functional guidance of outplacement activities through the organization.

    b. Select the outplacement consulting firms to be utilized by the Corporation.

    c. Be responsible for all policy and procedural aspects of outplacement activities.

    d. Provide training and orientation to all employees in the organization who have a responsibility in the outplacement process. Each operating unit of the Corporation shall designate an Outplacement Representative, who will assume responsibility in that organizational component for outplacement activities. That representative will be functionally responsible to Corporate Human Resources.

2. Line management, through the Performance Appraisal Review process, is responsible for assessing the individual employee's present and future abilities and desires, and when these cannot be accommodated/integrated within the organization, to recommend appropriate action. When that action results in a request for outplacement assistance, the outplacement representative, in conjunction with the line manager, will determine the extent of services that will be provided to the individual. Details of an individual's separation, including outplacement services and support and designation of a counselor (internal or external) will be developed by the responsible manager and the outplacement representative in line with all appropriate policies and procedures.

3. A *confidential* activity report will be prepared on a monthly basis by the

responsible outplacement representative for Corporate Human Resources with a copy to the responsible manager.

Training—Key to Termination's Effectiveness

A key to effective terminations in any organization is preparation. To be prepared in this volatile and litigious work environment requires an increased emphasis on training of the responsible managers. It may require a new philosophy about training in many organizations. Such a philosophy should reflect that training relative to terminations is a dual responsibility. The major areas needing attention are the critical parts of the linkage: hiring, appraising, and terminations. Training for these areas should be done inhouse. Outside training will probably not understand or project the needed sensitivities to the subtleties and nuances of each organization. One exception may be training for the firing manager. An outplacement consultant will often bring unique insights to this problem.

Training in these areas must become the rule and not the exception. It can no longer be thought of as a necessary evil (something Personnel does). It must be considered an integral part of the sustenance of the organization. Training is not a luxury to be conducted when time can be squeezed out of busy schedules. Employment-at-will implications alone should indicate that. This training must be put in the context of prevention: that if done well, less monitoring of practices will be required and fewer termination-related problems encountered.

Training in termination techniques speaks directly to earlier discussion of manager training: a manager is a manager when he or she understands and implements the interpersonal skills required to hire, appraise and terminate employees effectively. The need for this training goes back to some basics:

Most managers have yet to understand that they are also HR managers—they really make the people decisions.

Because they don't understand their role, they usually don't hire well and often abdicate responsibility for effective performance appraisals and terminations.

Most managers have yet to understand that it's not what is done in terminations but *how* it is done that determines their effectiveness.

Organizations and managers don't like controversy or conflict; thus the subject of terminations makes a book like this necessary.

The training ideas that follow are the author's own, and he doesn't profer any particular talent in the field of training. The techniques are left to the experts. This text will specify the particular subjects needing attention. It is hoped that other chapters of this book will provide the information for the expert (the HR manager) to develop specific training scenarios. Emphasis will need to be on practicalities: What are the potential problems? What are the hidden agendas? What are the internal political implications? What level of effort and commitment will it really require to do the job right?

The Employment Process (Hiring)

In some ways this may be the most critical and complex, because it is the beginning of the cycle for every employee. If done well, it can minimize problems in the other pieces of the linkage. Bad employment practices eventually cause terminations. Bad employment practices will improve when managers accept responsibility for decision making. Training in this subject matter should focus on defining the subject, defining needs, selecting the right person, and orientation (getting started right).

Define the subject—Everyone understands "employment," but no one does; it isn't just "hiring." Hiring is only one piece of the puzzle, albeit an important one. Employment, in its finest definition, is, however, a threefold process:

1. *recruitment*—utilizing all available resources to identify candidates and develop their interest as potential employees;
2. *selection*—through interviews, reference checks, and assessment of various types, arriving at the hire/not hire decision; and
3. *placement*—inducting, introducing, and *orienting* of the new employees.

The training message to emphasize about recruitment should be: don't start until you know what you need. You will fail without the proper definition. Without the proper definition, you will misutilize or underutilize manpower resources. Asking the right questions at the beginning will improve the odds that the process will attract the right person:

Why do we need this job/person? Is it really necessary?

Do we have someone internally who can do this job?

What do we want the person to do?

What results do we expect them to achieve?

What characteristics and skills must they possess to be able to understand and cope with our culture and environment?

Failure to consider these questions poses several inherent dangers. By not ascertaining why the person is needed, and specifically for what, the organization tends to get fat, causing terminations somewhere down the line. Most larger organizations are overstaffed because they overhire, particularly when times are good. Being a lean organization just to be lean isn't necessarily the answer, but being lean with the right people is. Good employment practices are the best insurance that the right person will be hired. Furthermore, not asking the right questions often results in hiring someone overly specialized—someone who may meet an important, immediate need, but will be surplus as soon as the crisis passes. Faced with this type of manpower demand, more organizations consider consultants or part-time temporary help.

Once the decision is made that the job does indeed need to be filled, the next important step is to develop realistic job descriptions/specifications. To achieve realistic descriptions, the following factors should be considered. First, you seldom hire the exact person you start looking for. There is almost always some compromise. You must determine what is *really* needed in the position—the absolute requirements and the desirable qualifications. What do you need in the employee to meet all of the job objectives set?

A second factor to remember is that everyone hired should not be from the same mold. Too many organizations are "clonal hirers"—that is everyone has the same education, background and experience. This may impact heavily on the organization's innovation, creativity and growth.

Finally, inability to work with one's boss is a leading cause of turnover. That makes it imperative that the chemistry requirements be factored in— the interpersonal qualities required.

The descriptions must always be job-related, as called for by EEO legislation. It is judicious, in light of employment-at-will implications, to have a disclaimer on the job description form that states: "These are not the only or total parameters of the job. One can be asked to perform other duties."

A comprehensive, accurate and reasonable job description will expedite the selection of one candidate from many. It will be a valuable aid in the training and development of the new employee, and it will serve as the cornerstone for performance appraisals. The description is an integral part of documentation should there be litigation concerning an individual who raises an issue as a candidate or terminee.

To *select* the right person, the decision maker must have the patience to find the real person. The real person is not just what the particular candidate wants you to perceive about themselves; what are they really? To develop the patience necessary, it should be emphasized in training that most people feel they have inherent skill at sizing up other people. That belief often results in very subjective judgments and bad hires. Furthermore, a manager should understand what it costs to hire and what it costs to fire. That knowledge will foster patience.

Managers need to learn how to measure the "can do" and "will do" of the job candidate. Good selection does not just measure the individual's ability to do the job; that is the easy part. Ability assessment measures past performance and accomplishments, evaluates skills, abilities and experience. Measuring the past is important, because the past is still the best predictor of the future. However, the critical part of selection (and a major factor in hiring failure), is measuring *will* they do the job? This is difficult because it means assessing the individual's motivation, style, and determination to compete and be successful in a particular organization environment. Can the candidate understand the subtleties involved in working here? What is the chemistry between the candidate and the organization and the boss? A definition of the chemistry needs of each particular job *must* be made in the description. Michael W. Nees also recommends answering the following questions to predict good matches:

What are his or her interpersonal, intellectual, managerial, and physical styles?

What are his or her likes and dislikes?

What are his or her beliefs and values?

Corporate culture provides a behavioral profile of the organization for the potential employee. On the other hand, the potential employee must also have his or her behavioral profile weighed against that of the hiring manager. Yet, as Nees says: "It is seldom that 'personal chemistry' is formally stated or defined in a job specification. This is difficult, but well worth the time and effort to measure the hiring manager in relation to interpersonal, intellectual, managerial and physical style. What are the likes and dislikes? What are the beliefs and values?"[20]

The organization that develops a chemistry criteria in its job specifications will have greater success in finding the best candidate for the job. If selection is not considered in this light, the organization may only do "clonal hiring." Hiring results in an organization where everyone went to the same (or the *right*) school, dresses alike, has the same experience, and so on, leads to a distinct lack of creativity and innovation, and the hiring of the wrong people—who end up as terminees (often in short order).

Another critical and too-often overlooked part of effective selection is providing enough exposure by the organization to the candidate, and by the candidate to the organization. This can't be stressed enough in training. The more the two parties (employer and candidate) know about each other, the better the odds for success. The effective organization utilizes all the tools and techniques available when recruiting to improve the odds that, when a decision is made and an offer extended, it will work.

Dan White, director of manufacturing at Freon Pharmaceutical, a $3.5

billion company, needed to hire someone for a newly established position of manager of manufacturing quality. It was an important job which would report directly to Dan, who was a capable, thorough, detail-minded man, albeit structured.

Freon engaged an executive search firm to find candidates for Dan, and the firm had several meetings at Freon with Dan to get a fix on the organization and to spell out the job specs. The third candidate who was recommended to Dan, Norm Alden, had excellent credentials in the industry, in addition to a stint in consulting. He was a very bright, analytical, inquisitive, entrepreneurial young man. The selection process moved rapidly, references were checked and they jibed with interview inputs, and an offer was extended. Norm accepted about a week later and reported to work.

It was about six months to the day that Norm reported that Dan decided to release Norm. When queried, Dan said: "The chemistry just isn't right. He's bright, quick, and so on, but he just doesn't fit."

What went wrong? It all started with a lack of attention to developing a behavioral profile of Dan—the chemistry measure. Dan and Norm were really poles apart. Dan was highly structured and liked to work in a highly organized environment. No one had paid much attention in interviews to Norm's entrepreneurial bent. As a matter of fact, it was intriguing in a sense, because Freon was a ponderous, if successful organization, and Norm may have appeared exciting because Freon was so staid. Charisma overcame reality. Norm wasn't on board very long before he began rocking the boat. He was full of ideas and like many bright, entrepreneurial people, had little patience with people who didn't think or operate the same way. He was so bright and personable that he had overwhelmed the selection process, but he was far removed from Dan's chemistry in the everyday world of work. Both sides should have recognized this, but because Freon and the search firm failed to measure the chemistry ingredient, Norm was out of a job.

Donald Allerton of Allerton Heinze Associates makes the point well: "without understanding that the job candidate must be compatible with the macro-environment in which they will be a new employee—the corporate culture, as well as the micro-environment—the chemistry requirements of the hiring manager, the relationships will probably go bad."[21] That almost always results in termination!

What *is* the chemistry factor that is so crucial to the selection of the right person for the job? A particularly good insight is provided by Dr. Nees and should be included during training. He suggests chemistry is of crucial importance in the selection process because:

> Primarily it plays a significant role in a candidate's eventual success in an organization. The inability to work well with one's boss is one of the most crucial elements of overall fit into the organization, and a leading cause of

turnover. Consequently, predicting the candidate's chemistry match with the hiring manager should be an important part of any selection. This is paradoxical because one seldom finds "personal chemistry" formally stated or defined in the position specification, despite its importance. . . . Personal chemistry refers to the feelings that arise between individuals as they interact in the business setting. Are they positive or negative? The more positive the interaction, the more comfortable the two people will be working together, and the more they will facilitate one another. "Hitting if off," "on the same wavelength," and "taking a liking to," are some of the colloquialisms we use to describe this type of relationship.[22]

Predicting the right chemistry is extremely difficult, even though it may be seen as two people interact. There is no set pattern for predicting it; very *different* people can have excellent chemistry. Many hiring managers feel that everyone should have "good chemistry" with them; that may be a fallacy. Harmony between the two is necessary; a high degree of compatibility is not. If that is not understood, managers may overlook qualified candidates who could make important contributions. To improve the interview/selection process:

Use the interview is a time to gather new information, not to rehash the facts already known (resumé, application form, etc.).

Do not process any more people than necessary. The risk grows as more people are seen that something will be done wrong.

Keep all interviews on a professional level. The dialogue must relate to the job in question and not stray into unrelated areas. (That's when litigious things get said.)

If you use interview evaluation forms (they provide a record of hire/ don't hire decisions), be sure that dangerous remarks are avoided, for example, "not too bad an engineer for an older guy." (See exhibit 1)

Don't oversell in interviews. Don't say things to be regretted later; make no promises about the future.

In turning down candidates for a particular job don't try to be helpful by being too specific, for example, "We found someone with the same experience but they are younger and hold greater potential"; "We felt it would be more comfortable all around not to hire a woman at this point." You don't have to say anything more than "We feel we hired the best candidate among those we had to select from."

Placement and orientation; don't blow it now. Of all the pieces of the linkage, orientation may be the most misunderstood or understated in terms

Exhibit 1: Interview Evaluation

Candidate _____

Position considered for _____

Knowledge (is he/she technically qualified? Know enough to get the job done? Considering such factors as education, prior experience, and record of achievement to date, should he/she be able to function in this assignment?)

CHECK ONE: COMMENTS:

☐ Particularly strong

☐ Adequate

☐ Doesn't meet minimum requirements

Skills (Will he/she be able to successfully apply know-how? Considering such factors as intellectual and problem-solving ability, communication skills, social awareness, etc., is there enough developed capability to function in this environment?)

CHECK ONE: COMMENTS:

☐ Particularly strong

☐ Adequate

☐ Doesn't meet minimum requirements

Attitudes (What is personal style—for example, confident? Considering such factors as initiative, willingness to work, aspirations, flexibility, self-insight, and sensitivity to people, how would he/she be likely to respond to the demands and rewards of the job—how would he/she be likely to behave in this environment?)

CHECK ONE: COMMENTS:

☐ Particularly strong

☐ Adequate

☐ Not well-suited

Summary comments and recommendations (Please express any other thoughts you have about this candidate's employability and future prospects with ACME)

Would you employ this candidate?

☐ Yes   ☐ No

Interviewer | Date

of importance. The point here is that a lot of time, energy and money have been invested in the newly hired employee. This is not the time to let them down or ignore them. New employees forgotten now may be casualties in the near future. The emphasis should be:

- Make sure that orientation is more than a one-hour lecture on benefits and company history the first day.
- Conduct orientation over a period of time, so there is an opportunity to absorb the information necessary to understand the subtleties of the organization's culture.
- Define the specific responsibilities for the HR manager and the practicing manager. (For example, the HR manager explains the benefits and organization rules. The practicing manager provides the real introduction to the culture of the organization and what it "believes in," and administrative details of the operating components like expense accounts and travel arrangements.)

Exercise discretion when explaining benefits in light of employment at will. Don't say, for example, "When you retire from XYZ . . ."; better to say "If you retire from XYZ,. . . ."

Performance Appraisals

Training for performance appraisals must be directed to developing and always improving the conduct of appraisals—developing good practices. These practices ensure that:

Appraisals are being done correctly.

Appraisals comply with organization policy.

Appraisals are completed before compensation is resolved.

Employees understand that performance counts and policy is real.

Managers inform employees of the importance of appraisals to compensation, promotion or any personnel actions.

Effective performance appraisal programs recognize the line manager as the quality control point and the HR manager as the monitor to ensure adherence to policy. The training scenario must spell out the major responsibilities and who must assume them. There are really three groups of people how must be involved and have the right degree of commitment to make any performance appraisal program effective: top management, practicing managers, and the human resources manager. As outlined below, each must assume specific responsibilities, at a minimum, if the true potential of an organization is to be measured and most effectively utilized.

Top Management

Responsible for developing the overall plans and programs to support the business objectives of the organization

Responsible for defining operational objectives in conjunction with their managers and for establishing standards of performance

Responsible for ensuring that evaluations based on accomplishment of objectives and performance standards are effectively utilized in making the decisions about promotion, compensation increases, or possibly termination

Above all, responsible for understanding the critical importance of the appraisal/evaluation program in detail, and communicating that commitment, understanding and interest throughout the organization.

Practicing Managers

Responsible for developing realistic objectives and performance standards for the people for whom they are responsible, in support of the overall objectives for the operations they manage

Responsible for ensuring accurate and timely inputs to employees concerning overall performance

Responsible for counseling employees honestly and objectively to foster improved performance and further development of capabilities

—Provide compensation increases and/or opportunity for advancement

—Initiate activity for termination if so required.

Human Resources

Responsible for administering the program under the direction and guidance of top management

—Ensure compliance with the program's objectives throughout the organization

—Devise, revise as necessary, and distribute the appropriate forms. Compile information and report on a specified schedule to top management.

Responsible for providing training in career counseling and termination techniques as necessary to managers.

For evaluation/appraisal systems to work, there must be an in-depth understanding of each employee's responsibility. The manager's role is to be sure all the reasons for and objectives of the program are spelled out in detail. People must know (and in reality, *like* to know) specifically what is expected of them. The more any of us knows about what we are to do or not do, the better the odds that we will do it well. The more employees know about job duties/responsibilities, the better they know how they will be evaluated and what they will be measured against. Knowing the responsibilities and expectations permits more efficient and thus, more effective work.

When jobs are truly defined in all their aspects, and good communication exists between manager and employee, the appraisal system will work. It must work if the organization is to be successful. In a successful organization, individual employees know where they stand and that what they contribute is meaningful and appreciated. That's what working is all about—people work harder when there is recognition. Ego is a great thing when massaged, and everyone responds and will even stretch a bit to do more and to do better when their accomplishments are recognized. Even when an appraisal is negative, helping the individual recognize why it isn't working is a plus. People can always handle failure better when there is an opportunity to learn something.

When termination for performance is the only answer with an employee, precise and definitive information must be available to document the action. What is said must be the rationale for the discharge, and always based on objective criteria. One key to effective administration of performance appraisals will be consistency, with respect to what is discussed/reviewed in any subsequent conversations with the individual about performance, objectives, etc. A good perspective for this might be to think of it as a performance improvement discussion, which means the emphasis should be on career planning. It might be better to call it a "performance and career planning review" to reiterate the "employment obligation" assumed when the employee is hired. Finally, according to legal experts Day, Berry and Howard:

Organizations should review their performance appraisal procedures with the following in mind:

a. Appraisals should be based upon objective criteria.
b. Stated grades of performance should permit the supervisor to recognize unsatisfactory to exemplary performance.

   c. Supervisors should be encouraged to use performance grading to differentiate among employees, not to give them equal or similar ratings.

   d. A section should be provided for the supervisor to discuss the principal weaknesses and strengths of the employee in narrative form.

   e. The appraisal should be reviewed by a higher level supervisor and the employee.*

   f. Supervisors should be instructed to be completely candid in preparing the appraisals.

*Additionally, one court has held that, where an employer undertakes to conduct performance reviews of its employees and fails to advise an employee of recognized performance problems that subsequently lead to the employee's discharge, the employer may be found liable for negligence. (*Chamberlain v. Bissell*, 547 F. Supp. 1067 (S.D. Mich. 1982))[23]

Firing Manager Training

Firing manager training is a necessity in any organization, because there are psychological, legal, and very sensitive interpersonal factors involved. This training should be predicated on the information presented in this text, with particular emphasis on the termination checklist. The checklist should provide the basic outline for this training. Emphasis should also be on the psychology of terminating. When that is fully understood, the firing manager will be much better prepared to deal with the unpredictability that always exists in this emotional confrontation. The termination interview will provoke anger, fear, self-pity, and shock. The degree of anger and emotion will almost always be based on how well the interview is conducted. The objective of this training is to accomplish the termination with the least damage to *all* the individuals involved.

The best preparation for the firing manager is to understand the decision to terminate fully and to plan. Terminations should never be taken lightly, nor should anything assumed—this is one of the most serious aspects of any manager's job! Following some basic rules to help better prepare for the actual termination scenario.

Unless the situation is dictated by corporate authority, i.e. a reduction of *x* number of people for whatever reason, it will be prudent to discuss the situation with another knowledgeable, objective person.

Do a thorough analysis of all the facts of the termination—unemotionally.

Never terminate in a crisis—not in the "heat of the battle."

When termination is decided upon, don't second guess. Have the confidence that the decision is the right one.

Realize you may have to "hang tough," expect to be second-guessed. No one termination is accepted by everyone.

Plan the actual termination scenario but don't be too rigid—no plan is ever consummated exactly (there are too many variables in this type of emotional confrontation). The best thing about plans is that they can be changed.

After the actual termination, you will need to work at rebuilding the organization's credibility. Prepare to communicate good, factual information.

Practice for termination interviews by role playing. This will increase the firing manager's familiarity with all the details of the process and the various reactions that may be expected. A dialogue may be developed based on the Random Corporation scenario in chapter 1. Termination training's bottom line is that termination is a message to the rest of the organization and the world how you as manager conduct yourself with employees in this most delicate situation.

Three more topics regarding training have been touched on and should be explained in a little more detail. These three areas need to be brought to the practicing manager's attention through some orientation or training effort.

References

There are real dangers in providing or not providing reference information. Approximately one-third of the lawsuits initiated about terminations relate to reference requests. Reference requests have to be responded to, and it isn't as easy as stating that "we only provide verification of employment dates, salary and job title." It just isn't reasonable to assume that a potential employer will bypass getting definitive information before making an offer to someone who has been released by an organization. All managers must be oriented to the process of providing reference information. Although there is no foolproof way of handling this subject, the following thoughts should help minimize an organization's potential liability.

Have a plan, a consistent policy regarding what types of information will be released. Courts have upheld actions of the new employer against a former employer for false or misleading information.

Have the terminated employee sign a reference information release authorization, and tell him or her that responses to reference requests will be truthful and accurate.

With all phone requests for reference information, follow this procedure:

inquire if caller has permission from the former employee; ask for title and phone number of person calling, and call back to ensure validity of call.

Provide facts and ensure that caller understands that this is "your opinion."

Answer questions asked; *do not* volunteer information.

Avoid written statements if at all possible—written information is more dangerous without in-depth verification.

Caution should be the byword. References must be provided, but require much more attention than most organizations give them. Organizations are vulnerable, both when hiring and when firing, and the terminee must have references to consummate an employment deal.

Contracts

Many organizations, for whatever reason, are anti-employment contracts but will, on the other hand, make oral promises or agreements to entice a new employee or retain an employee. The point is that oral agreements are often enforceable—are legal contracts when a burden of proof is satisfied (the whole thesis of employment at will is "implied contract"). A written job offer, of course, is also a contract when the offer is accepted, so care must be taken in how the offer specifics are stated in the letter, e.g., salary in weekly or monthly terms (*not* an annual amount). The wise organization considers contracts as one way to balance the organization's needs for confidentiality with the needs of an employee for mobility.

The increase in mergers and acquisitions in particular has made more individuals worry about their careers and tenure; and organizations, with pressures to compete effectively in this worldwide economy, worry more about the possibility of losing key employees to the competition. This has resulted in more people asking for some form of protection—something in writing. If promises are to be made in an age of litigation, they must be in writing. When put in writing, the odds are greater that they will adhered to. Both parties have a degree of security, and the parameters of the job (responsibilities of the position) can be defined. That, in turn, allows standards for performance to be specified.

For the organization, the biggest value of a contract may be its use as a recruiting and retention tool for good people. It allows the organization to say, "If you do this, we do this." It can solidify the employment obligation; both parties know exactly where they stand. If an organization is going to utilize employment contracts, procedure must specify who reviews and approves the final product. Legal advice is an absolute necessity here for both parties to the agreement.

There may be a wide variation in the elements included in employment contracts, ranging from expansive "golden parachutes" to relatively basic documents that spell out termination provisions. The guiding philosophy behind drawing up any employment contract is that it is a mutually advantageous situation, and to be effective, should not be viewed as one-sided by either employer or employee. An important element, particularly with technical and scientific people, will be a non-compete clause and protection for secret and proprietary information. (Many organizations have a separate document that all professional/exempt employees sign that specifies the rules vis-à-vis proprietary and secret information.)

Still, most employment contracts today tend to be fairly basic documents, as opposed to those written for more senior management levels, which may have a dozen pages of detail. The basic tenets of any employment contract are:

1. Terms/Length of the agreement—how long the obligation will last; the time frame (most are in the three- to five-year range)

2. Specifics about position/job responsibilities and title

3. Compensation details—base salary and review date; bonuses; other incentives, for example, stock

4. Benefits—insurance (medical, dental, etc.); pension; profit-sharing

5. Termination details—details outlined for specific circumstances, e.g., with cause, takeover

6. Non-Compete clause—specific parameters (time, geography, industry)

7. Proprietary and confidentiality ground rules—obligations of each party

8. Arbitration—rule for individual and organization to settle, or injunction rights if proprietary/confidential information dispute

There should be no reason for an organization to be offended or defensive when the question of a contract is raised during employment negotiations. It allows both parties the opportunity to talk openly and objectively about goals and expectations; it is a golden opportunity to solidify the relationship. It is the ideal way to start the employment relationship by spelling out the ground rules for both sides, and is a solid demonstration of both sides' commitment to "make things work" for their mutual benefit. It is a major step toward a successful relationship, and should be viewed in that positive light, not as an "us against them" confrontation. It is a most positive tool, and something an organization "can do."

Contract of Release

A new type of contract, a "Contract of Release," is being utilized by more organizations. This is a document that exists to gain agreement that an individual employee being terminated will not initiate litigation, and the employer will provide money or extra benefits to the employee. As long as the organization feels it is justified in terminating an individual, this contract can be proposed to the employee. However, it is a sensitive issue, because the employee must not feel he or she is being coerced into signing. However, when handled in a professional manner, this can eliminate a very sensitive issue.

Communication

Good communication involves openness and honesty with others. For any type of working relationship to be productive, communication must be open. People willing to level with one another are able to listen, recognize, and understand each other's needs. They are better able to minimize misunderstanding. Misinformation on any aspect of terminations can cause irreparable harm that may have long-lasting effects on employee relations and morale, as well as the organization's reputation as an employer. The latter is an important point, because the odds are that there will be a need to recruit new employees at some point in the future. So, credibility about terminations must be established within and without the organization. There must be a willingness to talk about it.

A good case to make the point in training is that of Meridien Chemical Company, which faced the first real economic crisis of its existence. Meridien had always been a leader in its particular product line, a company that could attract good people, a company that placed a good deal of emphasis on public and community relations. The problem now, however, was one that, unfortunately, dictated a major reduction in payroll, in addition to several other belt-tightening moves. Tom Green, the CEO of Meridien, met with the Management Committee, which included Ben Treadwell, vice-president of personnel. He said: "Our obligation to employees does not end with their involuntary separation. This obligation was part of the responsibility we assumed when we hired these people." Tom's message to Ben was even more succinct: "I want to ensure that all of the people affected are provided every possible assistance to aid them in making the transition to a new job." Ben recognized that the problem transcended just the people to be terminated. He was also responsible for the campus recruitment activities which covered schools from coast to coast. He was aware that many of Meridien's plants and facilities were in areas where they were a prime factor in the local economy. He was also quite sensitive to the professional societies to which so many of Meridien's employees belonged to, like the American Chemical Society (ACS) and American Institute of Chemical Engineers (AICHE).

Ben formulated a plan of action. His first thought was relative to all the good people they had hired over the years who would *not* be affected by the reduction. In some ways, they might be the most vocal critics of the reduction, with concurrent loss of confidence in the leadership, and doubts about the objectives and goals of the organization. They certainly would be more vulnerable than ever to inquiries from third parties and competitors. The approach with those who remained was to give them attention through good communication. Fortunately, Meridien was a company that had always communicated well and was known for that in the industry. It was astute enough about employee relations to recognize that employees have a right to know what's going on in all aspects of the business. It recognized that its continued well-being as an organization in an increasingly competitive world market made it imperative to communicate with all of its audiences, internal and external. Meridien felt strongly that employees have a right to know the good and the bad. Employees develop a sense of involvement when they know what's going on; morale is better. The message communicated to employees was that industry conditions (which were well publicized in the media) necessitated a reduction of costs, and in addition to various cost-cutting procedures instituted, a reduction in staff was being undertaken. This was elaborated on by a message from Tom Green to the effect:

> Our obligation to our employees does not end with their involuntary separation. We feel a responsibility for our employees' well-being even after we can no longer use their services. This responsibility is part of the obligation assumed by us when we hired persons we must now terminate. A program of assistance has been developed which includes outplacement counseling, readily available severance and vacation pay, and explanations of all details and options of benefits, pension, etc., to ensure that these plans may be utilized by employees to their best advantage. As we move through this period of change, I want to reassure everyone that the future is secure and the organization's vitality is unimpaired, and opportunities for growth for the business and individuals remain intact.

Ben's next area of concern was the campus. The campus was not only a major supplier of people, but a major factor in image-building—developing attitudes about the industry, the company and business in general. Because a number of the people affected were recent graduates, Ben asked several of his key recruiters to visit the campuses who supplied those individuals. The message was honest and direct: "We had to make the move for very rational business reasons and we are providing excellent support to assist these individuals to move to new positions. We used objective selection criteria in deciding who would have to go, and we are very optimistic about the future and the opportunities for growth for both the business and individual employees." The objective was to maintain the relationship with this most valuable resource by being direct and honest. Even though the campuses were concerned about the impact on some of their graduates, they were most appreciative of the personal effort made to keep them informed.

Ben was called by the American Chemical Society even before he could contact them. They were concerned that some of their members were impacted and *suggested* it would be advantageous if Meridien would elaborate. Ben assured them that Meridien was concerned, and suggested a meeting to elaborate. The ACS accepted, and an opportunity was presented for Meridien to spell out, in detail, what it was doing, and the support being provided. The ACS was pleased and featured an article on Meridien's approach in a subsequent issue of their magazine, *Chemical Week*. The article was a feather in Meridien's cap, inasmuch as it presented them as a concerned and humane employer.

Ben coordinated a communications effort, utilizing the Meridien Public Affairs Department, to provide each of the company's plants and facilities with the necessary information for use in those communities with local media, the chamber of commerce, etc. Each plant and facility appointed a spokesperson who served as the focal point for questions, and as the designator of information for the local press. Even though the staff reduction at Meridien was a traumatic event (as all of these situations are), the overall impact was greatly reduced by Meridien's attention to the details and the willingness to communicate openly.

Many organizations don't feel that anyone needs to know when there are termination problems: "we don't have to air our dirty linen." To the contrary, communication is everyone's right. The wise organization understands that and shares information, good or bad. It's true with any type of communication, but doubly sensitive with terminations—if you don't provide the real and timely facts, the employees and the public will get it somewhere else and it will probably be distorted.

Summary

An apt summary for this chapter is to list the steps that Paul Grossman, a Los Angeles attorney, suggests employers take to minimize their involvement in wrongful termination suits; and to maximize their chances of winning, should legal action be involved.

1. Review and rewrite all relevant documents, such as personnel manuals and handbooks, to remove any wording that could be construed as a guarantee of permanent employment.

2. In defining the company's standards for termination, cite specific examples of offenses requiring disciplinary warnings and offenses warranting immediate discharge.

3. Include in employment application forms a disclaimer making it clear that the company will not be bound by any oral promise of a duration of employment or termination standards.

4. Make sure that annual employee evaluations are realistic, so that in a trial, they will support the company's allegations about the employee's performance.

5. Use a disciplinary system with a specified number of warnings for each kind of offense. Keep a record of all offenses and warnings.

6. A corporate rule should specify that no supervisor has the authority to fire an employee without getting clearance from a designated executive, preferably a lawyer or knowledgeable personnel manager.

7. Before deciding whether to dismiss a particular employee, conduct a detailed review of all relevant facts, including consistency of treatment in that case and in the handling of all comparable cases.

8. Hear the employee's side of the story and take detailed notes before making a final decision on discharge.

9. Conduct the actual dismissal interview as privately and pleasantly as possible, and tell the employee the actual reason for discharge.

10. Obtain the employee's signature on a release from further financial and legal obligations, in exchange for certain contractual benefits, such as severance pay.

11. Be sure all employees understand that they must not count on any oral or other unauthorized promises concerning employment or pay.[24]

7
Outplacement—The Newest Employee Benefit

lthough many of today's outplacement practitioners will suggest they were the founders of the concept many years ago, the business was actually conceived in 1968. A couple of innovative people believed that organizations would pay for assistance when terminating an individual; thus outplacement consulting was born. Initially, it was a service dedicated to the more senior executive being released toward whom the organization felt a degree of guilt. Today, outplacement is a service offered at all organizational levels for individuals and groups of people. From the two or three original firms, the business has grown to several hundred firms with new ones appearing with regularity. Gross sales of outplacement services will easily exceed the $300 million mark in 1988. As the business has grown and prospered, the reasons for its utilization have changed from purely "guilt" to more practical reasons, such as maintenance of good employee relations, the threat of litigation; and "Everyone does it! It's good public relations."

Outplacement is the final step in the termination process and as such, must be understood and practiced with the same professionalism given to other business activities. It can be a very valuable tool for any organization, for a variety of reasons that will be discussed in detail in this chapter. However, by its very nature and cost, it is a misunderstood and much-maligned subject. It is incumbent upon both the practicing manager and the human resources manager to gain an in-depth knowledge of the subject, since they will be the key to selecting and effectively utilizing outplacement services.

More and more, organizations are recognizing that by having an outplacement philosophy and capability, they can greatly reduce the emotion and trauma for everyone involved and affected by a termination. So, what is this often-misunderstood and thought-to-be-mystical process called outplacement? In its purest definition, it is a *service which provides terminated employees with the knowledge and professional guidance to approach the job market in a businesslike and disciplined manner in order to find and obtain a new position in a minimum amount of time.*

The Role of Outplacement

The primary role of outplacement is to prepare the individual terminated for all job search eventualities, to give them a competitive edge in the job market. An outplacement counselor's role is to provide practical, step-by-step, hands-on advice, working closely with the individual on the key aspects of job hunting, including but not limited to:

Establishing a close working relationship with the person to ensure the degree of self confidence and discipline vital to successful job hunting;

Gaining an acceptance of job loss;

Providing an orientation for the spouse about job loss and job hunting;

Conducting a comprehensive self-analysis;

Developing a party line and organizing references;

Developing objectives and formulating a job-hunting plan;

Developing a comprehensive yet concise resumé;

Developing necessary correspondence;

Providing insights into all job resources and effective utilization of each;

Providing insights into interviewing, including practice interviews;

Assisting in offer negotiations and checking out potential employers (is it the *right job?*); and

Providing insights into getting started effectively in new job.

Equally important, however, is mental and emotional preparation for job hunting, and consistent, ongoing support throughout the search. Outplacement helps the employer defuse hostilities about the former employer, regain self-confidence, set realistic goals, and maintain discipline and motivation. Volumes have been written about the values of outplacement to the individual and the organization, but the practicing manager and the HR manager need simply to understand that very few people know how to job hunt effectively. When a person is in as stressful a situation as termination, it is a big plus to have someone else worrying about the problem, too. That's really what the outplacement counselor is being paid for—to lead the individual through the maze of a job search.

How Does it Really Work for the Individual?

When Larry Cleveland, the controller, was terminated at Memory Science Corporation, he was offered outplacement assistance, as part of his severance agreement. In his naïveté and anger, Fred said: "I don't need any shrink to talk to me. I can find a job—I've never asked anyone for help in my life, and I don't intend to do so now." Fortunately, Marion Freidan, who was the staffing manager at Memory Science, had had extensive exposure to outplacement, and sat down with Larry and explained some facts of life:

"You would be foolish not to take advantage of this opportunity. To work with someone who is an expert in the employment/job-hunting process, just as you are at finance and related matters, would be a distinct advantage to you. Have someone else worrying about the problem of finding another position. At a minimum, it will provide you a greater comfort to have someone involved with you.

"By your own admission, you haven't looked for a job since you graduated from college. Even the two changes you made didn't require you to really look—to mount a full-fledged job search. They came about because someone approached you, and it was an easy transition. This is a different ball game; now *you* have to get out and make it happen in the most efficient and economical manner, and there are a lot of tricks of the trade that you don't know.

"You will definitely need to improve your interviewing skills (learn how to cope with being the interviewee) and to gain a much better understanding of yourself and your strengths and weaknesses. You have to be prepared to present yourself in the most positive manner to a potential employer. You have to learn how to market yourself.

"You, like most people, have minimal knowledge of the resources available for job leads, like employment agencies, executive search firms, networking. To use these sources effectively, you need to know the who, what, when, where, and why of each.

"You don't know much about salaries, incentive plans, relocation, and a variety of other things relative to a new job. Can you negotiate the best situation for yourself? Can you do an effective value analysis of an employment offer?"

"Your wife is going to have a lot of specific questions and concerns about what's happened and about why the process works the way it does—you could surely use some help in explaining to her and the family."

The points Marion put forth, fortunately, got Larry's attention, and he began to recognize how ill-prepared he probably was to tackle the task at hand. Also, it wasn't going to cost him anything; his employer was paying for the service. He decided he would be a fool not to take advantage of the service. By the next day Marion had introduced him to Jim O'Brien, who was a senior consultant with New Career Directions, an outplacement firm that Memory Science had utilized previously with good results.

O'Brien began the meeting with Larry by explaining what outplacement was and how New Career Directions approached the problem. The approach was a good one. Each individual was viewed as just that, an individual who had different needs, desires, problems than the next. The program was very unstructured; emphasis was placed where needed. It wasn't a program where one hour was devoted to this, two hours to that, but rather a program in which the appropriate time would be spent to solve the individual's particular problems. New Career Directions would tailor to the program Larry's individual needs.

Cardinal Rules of Job Hunting

O'Brien began an explanation of the program they would follow by telling Larry that there were some cardinal rules for job hunting, and these would continually be stressed throughout the job search, because they were vital in making things work the right way. O'Brien also made it very clear that there is no formula or one way to find a job. People are too complex, and the employment process as practiced in most organizations is negative, bureaucratic, generally inept, slow and disorganized, and this makes job hunting an extremely difficult and frustrating task. It is a task that will test the patience of the most patient, that will always take longer than anyone anticipates. To counter some of these negatives and to ease the frustrations inherent in looking for a job, O'Brien insisted that these cardinal rules should always be paramount in Larry's mind as he pursued his job search.

1. *Don't do anything yourself that you can get someone else to do.* This is the core rule of job hunting—this is what networking is all about: using one's personal contacts to develop other contacts to develop job leads.

2. *Don't believe anyone will do what they say they will.* Too often all the good intentions people have get lost in the priority of doing more immediate things. Follow-up is the name of the game for the job hunter.

3. *Always tell the truth and you won't have to remember what you said.* Few people are adept enough at lying to get away with it, over a period of time, anyway, so don't even try. Sooner or later the truth will come out, and you'll lose; so no games.

4. *Pay attention to the details and maintain a discipline about your search.* To get a leg up on the competition, pay attention to the little things, and don't shortcut anything. Set up a work schedule, preferably no different than your usual schedule, and stay with it even when you think not much is happening; that's discipline.

5. *Maintain a proper appearance and attitude and be aggressive.* The right appearance and attitude are key factors in the chemistry of hiring. We are judged by our appearance, so be professional. Attitude means being self-confident, positive and goal-oriented. Aggressiveness is necessary to

make things happen, to remove the usual apprehensions, to take the initiative.

The second point O'Brien made to Larry was that for outplacement to work successfully, that is in the most reasonable time frame, there must be a very open, honest relationship between them. There could be no games, no charades; all the cards had to be on the table. O'Brien stressed that there has to be good chemistry for the outplacement process to work most efficiently and economically. He summed it up this way: "The more I know about you, your values, your style, your strengths and weaknesses, the more helpful I can be. We are both working toward the same goal, to find the right job for you."

Larry was in perfect agreement about the relationship, but it was also obvious he was deeply hurt and concerned about the termination. Although he took a very stoic approach that "these things happen, and that's business," the circumstances were really grinding away at him. O'Brien began to probe a bit and finally pushed the right button—Larry almost broke down and said: "Look, I'm fifty-five years old and I don't have a degree. Who's going to hire me? My whole career is in shambles. What am I going to do? I have lots of obligations."

O'Brien's response was direct and logical. "How did you get to be controller at Memory Science? You had to have the skills and ability, and it obviously was recognized that you did. Don't you think you are good at what you do? If so, you can always do it someplace else. But, you have to believe in yourself—if you do you can accomplish anything." The message really was, have the right degree of self-confidence, and you can do or be anything you want to. One of the most critical ingredients in job hunting is just that. Self-confidence will counter most of the negatives, be they self-pity, age, lack of formal education, or whatever.

The Specific Steps

O'Brien then moved the discussion to the specifics of the program they would jointly put in effect. They talked through the various steps, always with the understanding that the emphasis would be placed where it was needed. Following is a review of that discussion.

1. *Assist Larry in accepting the job loss* both intellectually and emotionally in order to develop as rapidly as possible the positive attitude so necessary to begin the process and to be able to identify and communicate his skills, abilities and accomplishments to the marketplace. Until Larry accepts what's happened, he won't hear or be ready to move ahead in a meaningful manner. When he reaches the point of recognizing "what's done is done," then he will be ready to get on with his program and his career.

2. *It was suggested that Larry's wife might want some orientation* to the problem and the actual process. The spouse is usually the terminated individual's biggest booster, and a most positive force for them. But too often the spouse does not have a real understanding of why these things happen, nor of the severity of impact on the individual. Also, there is generally little knowledge of the time frame that may be involved, which may be the biggest factor in a spouse's mind (paying the bills; buying the groceries).

3. Help Larry in developing a *thorough self-analysis* covering business experience, salary history, educational background, strengths, weaknesses, attitudes and motivation. This information would be developed through an extensive interview covering Larry's whole life. This discussion included getting Larry and his wife to spell out their priorities: what is most important at this point in life in terms of job, career, family obligations? A good fix on these values is a major factor in setting goals and objectives.

The career or job options that Larry might have in mind would also be explored now, for example, buying a business, consulting, changing career fields. O'Brien impressed on Larry that now was the time to do some really reflective, introspective thinking about himself, to take some quiet time and do some honest, objective, self-evaluation. There would never be a better time to do it, nor would it probably ever be as meaningful.

4. Provide Larry with an *in-depth understanding of the vagaries of the job search process*—the nuances and subtleties, that when understood, would give him an edge on the competition. The crucial point here relates to an insight into the bureaucracy of the hiring process in most organizations, to understand the suspiciousness and subjectivity that is involved, recognizing the different sense of urgency of employer and job-seeker, etc. Understanding the downside of the process would make the search less traumatic for Larry.

5. *Develop an individualized job-hunting plan* with Larry based on his interest, functional expertise, aspirations, geographic considerations, compensation needs, and career options. This would be influenced heavily by Larry's geographic flexibility. Larry did not want to relocate for various reasons, and that automatically would impact his plan, because of the restriction on the number of potential targets (potential employers). In turn, that might impact compensation requirements, increased breadth of responsibility in a new job, and even future growth in worst case. Flexibility in looking broadly geographically obviously provides that much more potential opportunity. O'Brien impressed on Larry that he might well have to sacrifice something in job or career to achieve his goals of not moving.

6. Larry's next step would be to *develop a complete, concise, accomplishments-oriented resumé(s)* designed to generate interviews. First he would develop an understanding of the role of the resumé—that it doesn't get anyone a job; it exists really to open doors for a face-to-face interview; it must be factual, honest and supportive. Larry would have to develop a com-

prehensive list of his accomplishments over the years, action statements portraying him as an individual who had accomplished things, who had solved problems. The goal would be to develop a resumé that would open doors and make Larry stand out among the competition.

7. *Develop the variety of correspondence* necessary to conduct a successful job search. The experience level of the job hunter often dictates the volume and variety of letters that may be required, however, the same basic ground rules apply regardless of who the job hunter might be: letters should always be professional, grammatically correct, neat, and above all, concise yet factual. Larry fortunately was a skilled communicator, and this would pay real dividends in his job search, where so much hinged on the written word to key executives in various organizations. Good letters are one of the keys to efficient job hunting. Good letters have a better chance of being read in entirety, while poorly written ones, like most resumés, generally get rather cursory review.

8. Larry was provided *a definition of and orientation to all job resources:* third parties (executive search firms and employment agencies), advertisements, networking, cold contacts, etc., and the best approach to each. O'Brien would make lists of appropriate third parties available. He also assisted Larry in gaining an understanding of the various directories and publications that could be useful, such as Dun & Bradstreet directories; state manufacturer's directories; Standard & Poor's. Particular emphasis on resources was directed to networking—how best to utilize Larry's personal contacts. Networking, when done correctly, accounts for a majority of the eventual job leads uncovered by any job hunter. O'Brien stressed, however, that even in light of that, no one resource is a panacea; all must be utilized, and then decisions about priorities can be made when one begins to see results. He also made the point to Larry that the resource that might have worked for a friend might not work for him, but that he would get a lot of free advice. Everyone is an expert about the other guy's job hunt, and Larry would have to use his own good judgment to ensure the best use of his time.

9. A most valuable step would be preparing Larry for the interviewee's role in the interview process. This included detailed discussions of the selection process, with emphasis on the subjectivity of it, types of questions, types of interviews and interviewers, preparation techniques and how to follow through and follow-up. This would include role-play interviews (videotaped) and critique. O'Brien also made the point that after each interview, the two of them would conduct a debriefing, a critique. He also suggested that Larry read an excellent book about being an interviewee, *Sweaty Palms,* by H. Anthony Medley.[25]

10. O'Brien could provide *information on potential employers* and *advice on negotiating compensation packages*. O'Brien explained to Larry that there is an art to finding the "right job," the one that makes the most sense

based on goals and objectives. He said: "Larry, as individual situations develop, we will prepare a strategy to negotiate the best compensation situation and an approach to checking 'their' references, as they check yours. The objective is to narrow the odds that the situation offered is the right one, and if accepted, that it will be successful move." This involves a variation of a value analysis—sizing up what's offered against what one had previously and what one desires in a job at this point in time in the career.

11. Last but not least, *provide advice and counsel on how to get started the right way in the new job.* They would outline a proper approach to settling into a new environment without causing too many waves. How to get the "lay of the land" and get off to a good start by being sensitive to the little subtleties of the new organization, and how to deal with them.

These are obviously not all the points that may be covered in a program for an individual, but the list provides an insight into the major areas that must get attention. The degree and intensity of input into any one of those basic steps must depend on the individual's needs and desires if the process is to work efficiently and economically.

Having explained the procedure, O'Brien felt Larry was ready to move ahead in to the job search. Five months later, to the day, Larry accepted another controller's job with Foremost Electronics. It was a short commute and a larger company, with a better compensation package—and it was the "right job."

A Group Layoff

Sussex Manufacturing was facing a dilemma. Business had slowed dramatically, and it was the best judgment of management and the industry in general that there were several slow years ahead. The Japanese had had dramatic impact on the marketplace, and Sussex products just weren't moving; . . . sales and profits were way off. Charles Odrun, Sussex's president, agonized with the management committee over the problem. A number of approaches were considered, and it was determined that, unfortunately, there would have to be a reduction in work force. There seemed to be no other way out of the problem. Phil Bryant, vice-president of human resources, was informed of the decision and was directed to institute a program to move out two hundred exempt and nonexempt and hourly employees. Phil had not faced a problem like this before, but he had been given a charter by Charlie Odrun "to do everything possible to ease the transition for the people to be affected." Through his network, Phil identified a very capable outplacement consulting firm, Howard Daly Associates, and set up a meeting with the principals to discuss his problem.

After lengthy and detailed discussions, Daly Associates recommended a number of approaches as possible solutions to Sussex's problem. The first point was that any group outplacement program, like any other project, would operate more efficiently if some thorough planning was done before any actions were taken. For example, consideration must be given to such things as fair and equitable administration of policy; eligibility for recall; benefits; how best to communicate with all involved parties, utilization of internal resources versus external outplacement resources, or a combination of both; etc. Many organizations have human resources professionals who can assist displaced employees in their job search; however, there may be mitigating circumstances which dictate an organization's decision to "make or buy."

A key part of the planning, Daly pointed out, necessarily had to be the identification of employees to be terminated. Unfortunately, the best selection system for making these decisions is usually imperfect. This task often requires some real soul-searching and hard decisions. Daly stressed that one of the keys may be the effectiveness of the organization's employees who are not employed at will. What are Sussex's obligations by contract? The criteria Daly suggested related to five factors:

1. employee's discipline,
2. program on which employee works,
3. performance appraisal,
4. experience in general, and
5. overall capability.

Phil Bryant, in conjunction with the involved line managers, assumed responsibility for determining who would go, utilizing those basic criteria. Daly was very helpful to Phil in defining responsibilities for program administration and organization: primary responsibility would fall on the Human Resources department to organize and provide the direction to all activities associated with the outplacement program. The development of a termination checklist was given high priority to ensure none of the critical details would be overlooked, such as communication responsibilities and their timing.

Seminars and Workshops

In terms of specifics, Daly recommended group counseling in the form of seminars/workshops for personnel to be released. In addition, they also strongly recommended that some degree of follow-up counseling be planned after the seminars on a structured, one-on-one basis. This follow-up counseling was recommended to ensure that the information imparted in the seminars was effectively put into practice to move the terminated employees quickly and efficiently into the job market. Daly recommended a two-day seminar format for the exempt employees to best prepare them in launching an organized job search with positive action plans and well-defined objectives. For nonexempt and hourly employees, a one-day job hunting seminar was recommended.

Daly reviewed the many details involved in seminars of this type, because there will be variations from group to group, depending on a variety of factors, for example, level of the individuals, functional expertise, local job market. Daly also recommended that the seminar size be limited to not more than twenty-five people in order to allow a true workshop atmosphere, rather than a lecture format. Daly's final point on the value of the seminars was that for a group, the seminars are a big plus because of the involvement of *all* terminees, and the support that evolves from a "we are all in this together" attitude. Good seminars play a major role in tempering the ill feelings that always exist in any termination situation affecting numbers of people.

Placement Support Center

Then Daly recommended establishing a placement support center (PSC) to provide office facilities for the terminated employees for a period of time following the seminars. Fortunately, Sussex had a lease on some office space in town. It was conveniently located for all the people who would be affected, and with a little work (installing phones and word processing equipment) could be ready to function within two weeks. A major value of the center would be to provide a base of operations in a "neutral zone." The additional counsel on a one-to-one basis would allow for questions that individuals might not raise in the workshops, and questions that would certainly arise as job searches gained momentum.

The PSC would also make available the following services to the terminees:

preparation and typing of resumés and related job correspondence;

collation of a resumé book of available employees for mailing to an extensive list of potential employers;

mailing of individual resumés to potential employers;

telephone and duplicating privileges;

coordination and distribution of employer inquiries;

distribution of employment agency/executive search firm lists;

location of jobs through advertising sources;

pro-active sourcing with employers on potential jobs, including job fairs and open houses;

extensive research of the opportunities in the area and industry;

ongoing workshops to enhance the job search, including video interviews and spouse counseling, if desired;

follow-up on contacts, interviews and offers; and

library of "job source" publications.

This all made sense to Phil and Sussex, and they began to formulate their plans based on these ideas. It also was apparent that there were two other areas of concern that needed attention. Daly had suggested some training for the managers who would do the actual termination interviews to minimize potential problems inherent in that step. Daly also felt the outplacement program would be more cost-effective for Sussex if some of their human resources people could be made available for work in the placement support center (PSC) as counselors. Phil decided to implement both of these ideas, and arranged for a seminar for firing managers, as well as some in-house training in outplacement skills for several members of his human resources department.

Firing Manager Orientation

The orientation for firing managers at Sussex was based on the usual premise that while most managers are capable of hiring qualified people, many lacked the skills and understanding necessary to conduct an effective termination interview. With the employment-at-will concept being challenged more frequently in the courts, Phil felt it was imperative that managers develop this know-how in order to protect Sussex from possible litigation, and at the same time, preserve the rights and self-respect of employees affected as well as the reputation of the company. The orientation covered the dos and donts of firing, and led the managers through each step of a termination interview. It detailed such things as what documentation should be available, reactions to anticipate, the rights of the individuals. Specifically, the following points were elaborated:

What are the range of emotions that may surface and what is best approach to deal with them?

What will the firing manager feel and how to deal with that.

The structure of a good termination interview, and a review of potential litigious subjects.

Explaining the termination arrangements (benefits, severance, etc.) and how to follow up for details.

Explaining the value of outplacement services to be offered.

Security and medical arrangements.

A review of the typical questions and responses.

This training for managers was particularly important because, as Daly pointed out, this is often where even the best programs begin to fall apart. More often than not, affected employees say, "We can accept what has happened, but we are upset by how it was handled by the company." This type of orientation allowed a walk-through for Sussex's managers and prepared them with the knowledge and ability to perform this most difficult task more efficiently and with all the necessary sensitivity.

In-House Training

Phil felt that he indeed had the resources in his department to provide counseling assistance in the PSC but that some training was necessary. The training for in-house personnel was centered around understanding the psychology of firing, and the details of the actual job-hunting process as presented by Daly in the seminars. Phil knew there had to be continuity between the seminars and the ongoing one-on-one counsel provided in PSC to eliminate confusion and second-guessing of counselors.

The outplacement program put into effect was very successful for Sussex. The PSC was open ten weeks, and in that period about 90 percent of the nonexempt and approximately 55 percent of the exempt personnel had accepted new positions, with a majority of other terminees on the verge of offers or with interviews active and pending.

An Accepted Practice

As shown by the Memory Science and Sussex Manufacturing examples, outplacement is gaining stature with organizations faced with termination problems. Be they individuals or large numbers of individuals who are affected, outplacement consulting has become an accepted part of business culture. It has proven its value in literally tens of thousands of situations. Unfortunately, as much as it is utilized, there are still many misunderstandings about its value and practicality. This is primarily because outplacement is not a subject that most people want to consider except when necessary; it's the most negative part of their jobs! Also, there is still a constituency out there that cannot believe that a consultant needs to be paid when "we are getting rid of someone."

It should be helpful here to detail the rationale of outplacement and why it is an invaluable service when practiced with the correct degree of professionalism. The following are some of the basic facts of life about being terminated.

1. Most people profess or assume they have greater knowledge of the job-search process than they could conceivably have. It isn't a task performed often enough for the average individual to develop the needed level of expertise to accomplish it under what are often extremely stressful conditions, and to do it effectively and economically.

2. It must never be presumed that any one person or resource has all the answers about job hunting, but experience has revealed the methods that are the most practical and produce the best results, as well as those that generally are the least productive. The pitfalls to an efficient and economical job search are nearly identical for everyone, and the good outplacement counselor can provide an awareness of them.

3. Job hunting to achieve the proper results—the right job—must be approached as a business problem; it is a marketing/sales problem, in reality. In requires the same logic, commonsense, and decisiveness as in any other business problem. It isn't "something different" that will be solved in some mystical way. Individual patience, discipline and self-confidence must be the bywords, and a competent outplacement counselor can help bring that to each situation.

4. Time is the most valuable commodity for any job hunter. There is never enough, and it will almost always take more of it to accomplish one's goal of finding the right job than anyone believes. The practicalities of job hunting and the employment process are generally very misunderstood; nothing happens quite the way one thinks it does, or in the time frame it "should"! Professional guidance is a major help in making it happen efficiently.

5. An outplacement consultant does not get compensated for finding the right job for an individual. The consultants are paid for providing support and expertise about job hunting—the counsel, guidance, critique—and for easing the transition, but they are not in the placement business. They assist in solving the problem! They work through the process with the terminated individual—they counsel, they advise, they worry about it with them, which relieves to a degree some of the person's concerns and allows concentration on the critical things.

Why Outplacement?

Benefit to Organization

Outplacement as a management tool is both simple and complex for the organization and the individuals. First, the historical approach to terminations—pay them off and get them out!—is not longer acceptable. A positive approach is needed and outplacement provides this. The major benefits are:

1. It reflects an organization's concern for the terminated individual, which in turn fosters good relations with communities of interest. It says that the organization understands that it isn't necessarily the individual's fault that termination occurred, and proves that "we care and have a conscience."

2. It serves to improve employee relations with the remaining personnel, who might otherwise choose to leave or have diminished confidence in the organization. It boosts morale in the organization—"They really are helping those people who were terminated." It eases the trauma for those who remain, and provides a sense of security.

3. It minimizes the prospect of potential litigation which may arise from allegations of discrimination and other sensitive issues. There is an old saying in the outplacement profession that "people who are speaking to outplacement counselors are not speaking to attorneys about how they were mistreated!"

4. It effects a more objective approach to severance payments, which can often be excessive due to lack of other assistance.

5. It helps eliminate procrastination by management on separation decisions by providing a positive aspect—"We are going to assist you in making the transition to a new job."

6. It aids organizations by providing another tool for organizational development and growth.

Benefit to Individual

The major benefits for the individual are as follows:

1. It helps the individual gain acceptance of loss of their job, both intellectually and emotionally. Intellectually, a business decision has been made . . . right or wrong, it's done, and life must go on. Emotionally, it's important for the individual to recognize that it is a waste of energy to be angry . . . all effort should be turned to the job search.

2. It rebuilds the individual's self-confidence. Outplacement fosters an understanding that self-confidence is a key factor in job hunting, promotes a belief in self ("you wouldn't have achieved what you have if you weren't good").

3. It provides a thorough assessment of career direction. It assists the individual in engaging in some reflective and introspective thinking about what he or she has done (accomplished) and the tools (skills) available to do what he or she wants to. This includes an assessment of value systems, strengths, weaknesses, interests, etc. (This is an exercise that probably few people have done in their career because they were "too busy.")

4. It assists in developing effective job-search techniques. It helps develop an understanding that job hunting is a business problem, albeit a marketing problem, and will require the same degree of professionalism, understanding and attention to detail and planning to solve as does any business problem.

5. It effects a quicker relocation to a new position by providing ongoing counsel and critique as the job search proceeds.

The organization's belief in providing outplacement assistance very importantly allows employees to work more securely. This does not mean they will automatically feel that they have a greater degree of job security and will never lose their job; rather, they have the security that they will be treated fairly.

The outplacement posture of any organization will "get around" in employee and industry circles, and in all likelihood will be a plus in future recruiting efforts. "Yes, we did have to let some people go in 19XX, but circumstances were beyond our control, as you know. However, we provided full support as those people made the transition to new jobs." You become a "caring organization"!

Make or Buy

This is not an easy decision because of the complexities of each potential termination situation. There are good arguments for and against doing outplacement in-house as opposed to utilizing outside consultants.

Proponents of in-house services argue that:

there would be more individual counseling time available;

there is a better understanding of the individual and the organization/ environment;

there is more concern by the organization, because the terminee is still "one of them";

It is on-site evidence of concern to all the other employees.

Detractors point out that although most organizations have some competent human resources professionals who can assist terminated employees in a job search, circumstances often dictate the use of outside help and assistance:

The time, effort and individual follow-up required to provide effective assistance to a terminated employee are often greater than company personnel can reasonably allocate due to more pressing responsibilities.

The resources and experience of the outside consultant who deals exclusively in outplacement services are often broader than those found within the organization.

The employee is sometimes bitter and resentful toward the company. This attitude can usually be more readily dispelled by an objective third party.

Then there is a school of thought that says a combination of internal and external assistance makes the most sense. This has been an effective approach in many large staff reductions where in-house personnel supplement the efforts of outside consultants. The more senior and/or more sensitive individual situations probably should be handled by an outside expert, especially when there is a mature and knowledgeable counselor involved who can establish and maintain the level of rapport necessary. In the final analysis, there may be more objectivity and less emotion with an outsider. The need to dispel the feeling of enmity toward the company is always essential to getting an effective job hunt underway when inside people are involved.

Should the organization determine, for whatever reason, to provide outplacement only on an in-house basis, serious considerations and decisions must be addressed if a level of success is to be achieved. This is not a program that can be given lip service. Too much rides on the credibility of the organization to risk a half-hearted effort. If it cannot be given the same level of attention and support that any program critical to the organization would get, then it should not even be attempted without expert help.

Cost

Cost, of course, is a major factor, because it can be substantial, particularly when a senior executive is being displaced or it is a multiple termination. The caution should always be that one must look beyond the immediacy of the problem to consider the long-range implications before making the final dollar decision. As has been said, there are more considerations here for the organization than just helping the displaced person; there are many other factors involved that have far-reaching and long-term implications.

As in all businesses, costs vary in the outplacement consulting business—there are no hard-and-fast rules on what outplacement firms charge. However, a majority of the major outplacement firms charge a basic 15 percent fee for one-on-one counseling . . . predicated on the individual's total compensation (base + bonus). Most also charge a one-time administrative fee of $500–$1,500 to defray the costs of printing resumés, mailings, telephones, etc. Any travel and lodging expense incurred by the consultant on behalf of the client is also chargeable to the client organization. There has been a proliferation of firms in recent years and as expected, there is fierce competition; as a result, cost-cutting and various special fee deals may be arranged. Many outplacement firms will provide a fee discount where there is a volume of one-on-one candidates, for example, 15 percent for first three candidates; 12.5 percent for the next three; 10 percent for any over six in a specified time period. Also, a number of firms have arrangements predicated on a contractual basis, e.g., for the next twelve months, on an exclusive basis, we will handle all of your outplacement candidates for fees of *x* percent for individuals at this compensation level, and above *x* percent for the individuals at this compensation level and below. Most outplacement firms also have a minimum fee for individual counsel. For individuals below $30,000, a year it might be a $4,500 flat fee. Group counseling, in the form of seminars or workshops, is generally offered at a flat rate per attendee or per day for each assignment, plus expenses. Follow-up counseling in a PSC environment is generally charged on a per-counselor cost per day or week, plus applicable expenses.

A final word on cost. Granted, cost is always a factor in any purchase, but don't just buy the cheapest, because that often means just that—marginal service. Cheapness is often the best indicator of value received, and this is not a subject to be shortchanged, because of the number of interested parties.

Once the "buy" decision is made, a careful selection needs to be made. If an organization does not have a knowledge of firms available, a number of resources may be helpful:

The human resources department's own network into other organizations;

the Association of Outplacement Consulting Firms (AOCF), Attn.: Executive Director, 364 Parsipanny Road, Parsipanny, NJ 07054;

The *Directory of Outplacement Consultants,* published by Kennedy and Kennedy, Inc., Templeton Road, Fitzwilliam, NH 03477.

Firms have different capabilities; some are particularly adept at group work, others with senior executives.

Selecting an Outplacement Consultant

It behooves any organization to select an outplacement consultant with at least as much thought and attention as it would select any other type of consultant. Below are the critical points to consider in selecting an outplacement firm.

its ability to interface with the organization and exiting employees;

its knowledge of job market and the disciplines and job levels involved;

the background of the consultant(s) assigned to perform the actual counseling;

the specific responsibilities to be assumed by the candidate(s) and the consultant(s);

the levels and types of candidates whom the consultant has assisted previously;

the cost of providing the type of service that is required.

The company and/or the individual should consider a number of other important issues, and have a clear understanding of who is responsible for what prior to deciding on a particular outplacement firm. Answers to the following questions will be most helpful in developing the factual data for making this all-important decision.

Who will perform the actual counseling?
Because some firms use marketing representatives who sell the service, but are not actually involved in the counseling process, it is important to determine who the counselor will be. The critical point is that the right chemistry must exist between the individual terminee and the counselor—a mutual confidence and trust, if the situation is to reach a timely and successful consultation.

How long has the firm provided outplacement services to clients and how long has the counselor(s) been involved in outplacement?
Usually, it is more desirable to use an organization with broad knowledge and contacts; a company that has served clients in diverse industries, and is staffed with individuals who know and understand the vagaries of job hunting in detail.

What is the judgment as to the length of time that takes to conduct an effective job search?

The duration of the job search depends upon many factors, including: location, functional discipline, level of position, and compensation. The generally accepted rule is one month of job hunting for every $10,000 in salary; however, a major factor is the amount of time and effort the job hunter is willing to expend. Thus, there is no firm answer to how long the job search will take. A response that "all of our candidates find new employment in three months" should raise some questions!

How long will the counselor be available to the terminated employee?
Ideally, counselors should remain in close contact with the candidate for the *entire* time that it takes to complete the job search successfully.

Does the firm guarantee that it will find a new position for the candidate?
The primary role of the outplacement counselor is to prepare the candidate for all of the inevitables of the job search and to provide a competitive edge in the job market—to assist, not to find a new job. Outplacement is *not* a placement business like an employment agency or executive search firm. Therefore, no one can provide such a guarantee.

Does the outplacement firm make job contacts with potential employees?
Most organizations will place the responsibility solely on the candidate. Some firms have close relationships with many employers and employment sources and may be able to assist in contacts. The extent of the assistance to be provided should be understood fully prior to engaging any firm.

Does the firm provide office, phone and secretarial assistance?
This is crucial to the discipline necessary to conduct a job search effectively. These services should be *defined explicitly* prior to initiating any activity.

Does the firm have a testing capability? Does the firm have psychological counseling capability?
Although not services utilized with each and every candidate, these services should be available for use when needed. Find out who provides the services, and their credentials.

Does the firm provide any financial counseling service?
This will be invaluable in certain situations, and may be the crucial point in surviving the trauma of losing the job. The average person has done little or no planning in this respect, and now may literally have his or her back against the wall.

Is the spouse a consideration in the counseling?
This is too often an overlooked aspect of outplacement counsel. The spouse may have as many or different questions about the total impact, and certainly has individual concerns.

Does the firm espouse high professional standards of privacy and confidentiality and good ethical business practices?
Find out what professional organizations or associations the firm belongs to. What activities are individual members involved in?

What research materials and research capability are available for candidates of the firm?
Is definitive information available, for example, lists of employers and individual executives? What is the extent of the "library"?

Before finalizing the decision about a particular firm, ask for and check two or three references, that is organizations that have utilized the services of the firm recently, or individuals who have used the service. You are looking for an organization that has the expertise, that knows and understands corporate culture and mentality. You want an organization that knows jobs, the marketplace, compensation trends, has broad geographic contacts, etc. Ask good hard questions. How many resumés do you print? How many letters do you do? How is office space allocated? What progress reports would we get? The bottom line in choosing a consultant is to get "value received" for the fee(s) paid, and the desired level of professional assistance provided.

In most instances, certainly for any group counsel, the client organization will make the selection of the firm to provide the services. In some instances, however, the employer will give a terminated individual the responsibility for choosing an outplacement consultant. Because the individual usually lacks the knowledge and experience necessary to make such a critical choice, it often is better to suggest several firms that are well known to the organization and have the individual meet with them and decide who provides the greatest comfort level. Bear in mind, however, this is a difficult and confusing time for the individual, who is probably emotionally upset, and some guidance will be needed to ensure that they aren't being sold a bill of goods.

Above all, in selecting a firm to work with your organization, do as John Lucht suggests in his excellent book, *Rites of Passage at $100,000+*: "Be cynical! Look for a connection between what an outplacement firm recommends . . . and what their involvement in it costs them."[26] His message really came down to, "don't let ambiance be the competitive edge; what will they *really do* for you?"

Career Counselors

A distinction for an organization to make in considering outside assistance is the difference between an outplacement consulting firm and the career counseling firm. As this new field of helping people who lost jobs has mushroomed, it has logically attracted a variety of individuals with varying degrees of expertise and professionalism. It is not a business that has, as yet, set any definite professional standards, or necessarily requires any specific functional or technical credentials. The Association of Outplacement Consulting Firms has established some standards of professional practice, and, it is to be hoped, will continue to define standards and practices.

Probably the major distinction between outplacement consulting and career counseling is how the provider of services is reimbursed. Outplacement firms are paid by the *client organization,* who is releasing the individual(s); as opposed to the career counseling firms, which cater to both the organization, and unemployed individuals, who are obligated for the fee. There can always be extenuating circumstances, but experience would indicate that a good rule of thumb is to stay with the firms who *only* receive their compensation from organizations, not individuals. They are paid for the time and effort expended for a client—they are responsible to the client organization, as well as the individual, which may provide more control and assurance of positive results. The career counselor advocates, on the other hand, will counter that when the terminating organization is paying the bills, they receive no more negative marks than the outplacement consultants. There is a third piece to this puzzle; some (not many) placement organizations also work in outplacement and that poses a problem in many people's minds—where there may be a conflict, with two fees potentially involved.

A Plus for Managers

When outplacement is understood and accepted in an organization as a viable and credible concept, most employees will worry less about the "security" of their situation and be able to concentrate more fully on getting the job done. We are not implying that outplacement will do away with concern about job security, but rather that it can alleviate a great deal of anxiety. It has to offer some assurance to employees to know that the organization will help keep them "whole" while assisting them in finding another job. When outplacement is an accepted part of an organization's culture and personnel spectrum, it also provides managers with several very valuable tools. First, it gives them a method to make the performance appraisal process realistic. No longer do they have to stew about an abrupt severance of the relationship when the employee, for legitimate reasons, is to be terminated. They can be completely honest and objective about appraising and counseling an employee, because they have somewhere to turn. ("Kim, those are the reasons it's not working out here at XYZ. However, we are going to help you find another position.") Second, it establishes the credibility of managers and improves their rapport with employees. ("Any boss who would level with me can't be all bad. Those things we discussed are really what I needed to know to plan my career.") Finally, the bottom line of outplacement for the manager is that you can release people and let them handle their own problems, or you can help and meet your obligation and also allow the individual to "save face." It's just good business to help people for the many reasons discussed earlier. It's part of the employer/employee obligation that exists in any conscionable organization.

The Final Step

In summary, as organizations become more productive and efficient, they are recognizing they cannot "keep everyone." This has evolved into a much more active conscience on the part of many organizations to provide some degree of assistance in the affected individual's transition. It is the final step in the *employment obligation*. Because organizations wish to continue as vital and profitable enterprises, they are coming more and more to recognize that the cost of outplacement is less than not providing it under many circumstances. This is particularly true when outplacement prevents litigation by individuals or groups, and averts bad public relations and a tarnished image as an employer. Outplacement, by eliminating some of the usual managerial procrastination, saves time, which means money saved, in salaries and untold revenues that otherwise might not be obtained through inefficiency and nonproductivity. Outplacement has truly become a matter of social conscience; it's not only the right thing to do, it is sometimes a necessity to avoid litigation, like class action suits. Outplacement is beneficial to the company as a whole. It demonstrates in a most practical and realistic way to the remaining work force that the well-being of the employees is important. Without this kind of assurance, the solid performers—the ones you *don't* want to leave—may adopt an "it can happen to me" attitude and start looking for a new job.

8
Epilogue

There have been estimates that in the past decade, 1 million managers and staff professionals have lost their jobs for one reason or the other. A number of executive search firms have estimated that one-third of the middle-management positions in industry have been eliminated. A good deal of this action is attributable to the globalization of the market-place. There is no reason to believe that this trend will change. It may slow a bit, but there are still many fat organizations and poorly managed (in people aspects) ones, so it would seem there is no question that the problem of terminations will stay with us. There will never be a perfect solution to terminations, either, because of all the human factors involved in business and jobs. Things are much too complex, and human nature and human frailty will not change. Job security, as has been noted, does not really exist anymore in the classical sense. Job security will instead be the ability of the individual to hone his or her skills continually and be able to use them somewhere else when necessary. Security no longer means believing that the organization will keep the individual in a job as long as it is done well.

The message for the future is: the odds are high that people getting out of school today will change employers often during their career and in fact, may have second and third careers (careers in varied occupations). Because of mobility and flexibility, they will live in several different geographic areas, and will have, as the economy continues to globalize, a broader organization experience. They will increasingly be attracted to smaller firms.

As that philosophy takes hold, it will obviously pose problems for both employee and employer. For the employee, it will pose a greater problem of keeping up with the profession. He or she will be constantly under the gun to be improving skills and knowledge. The individual will also have to understand that there may be fewer jobs available for his or her interests and skills, and there will probably be more people looking for those jobs; that will make job hunting more difficult and may require more industry and career changes than in the past. New skills, or certainly broader skills, will be needed. Relocation may become a necessity to locate meaningful work. The individual may have a fundamental change in basic attitudes about work—the number one priority will be self. The organization will be less and less a factor in perpetuating one's career. The initiative more and more will rest with the individual to make a successful career.

If this is to be the scenario of the future, how should the concerned organization be prepared to respond? What must it do to minimize the impact of these changes? What changes need to be instituted?

Of major concern should be more emphasis on strategic people planning—finding, integrating, and using this, the organization's most critical asset. There must be a good deal more emphasis on the relationship between organization and employees. There must be more communication and involvement by everyone, but not to the point that management abdicates decision-making responsibility. All of the new participative management techniques are fine, but the buck still has to stop somewhere. Managers must get more training about how to do their jobs. Organizations must accept the fact that managing is not a title, it is a profession like many other things.

Managing will be an ongoing learning process, and will require a broader spectrum of skills. A good example is the theme of this book and the increased importance of knowing how to move people out of an organization under ever more stringent rules and regulations. Managers will have to be instilled with the philosophy that they are "part personnel manager," regardless of their primary function. Measurements must be conceived to let managers utilize people's skills to provide the greatest benefit to both organization and employee. Nathaniel Stewart puts it nicely in *The Effective Woman Manager:* "Management is a leadership effort aimed at integrating and using effectively the many resources entrusted to the manager."[27]

Organizations must change if they are to survive, just as people must. Industry's problems are not going away—foreign competition is here to stay and probably will be more and more of a problem. We know people's perceptions and attitudes about work have changed, and they will be more vocal regarding likes and dislikes about their jobs, and about how they are managed. Because an organization is only as strong as its people, they must be a party to change or it won't be successful.

Change for the organization also means that *lean* is the name of the game for the future. Not lean just to be lean, but lean because it's good business, because it's efficient. Change also means being willing to expend the time, effort and money to make people programs really work, particularly training and appraisal. There will be fewer people in organizations, so people programs must be good to maintain the needed level of productivity. There will not be room for those who cannot function effectively in the particular environment or within the corporate culture parameters; they will impede progress and must be relocated for their own good and the good of the organization. This must be done with no procrastination, but with genuine concern for the individual. A new corporate conscience will have to be evident about terminating employees. Pressure is building, and the odds are good that in the not-too-distant future, there may be career insurance, as there now is medical and dental insurance, for example.

Outplacement will truly be viewed as an employee benefit, something that is natural in an organization when things aren't working. The world of work is changing dramatically, and the organizations that will survive and be competitive and productive will be those who recognize the necessity of constantly reviewing, and when necessary, changing their approach to their key asset: people.

Notes

1. Gould, Richard. *Sacked! Why Good People Get Fired and How to Avoid It.* New York: John Wiley & Sons, 1986, 47.
2. Deutsch, Arnold R. *The Human Resources Revolution—Communicate or Litigate.* New York: McGraw-Hill, 1979, 2.
3. Coleman, Francis E., Esq. "Avoiding Wrongful Termination Lawsuits: The Employment at Will Doctrine and Its Exceptions," *Employment Management Association Journal,* Summer 1986: 3.
4. Riegel, Marilyn. "EMA Survey Describes Benefits Programs to Cushion Employees from Downsizing," *Employment Management Association Journal,* Summer 1987: 4.
5. J.J. Gallagher Associates. *A Report on Outplacement.* New York, 1979.
6. J.J. Gallagher Associates. *A Report on Outplacement.* New York, 1980.
7. Taft, Bradford H. "Employee Discharges Gain in Complexity." Talk given at the annual meeting of the personnel and Industrial Relations Association of California, Los Angeles, Fall, 1987.
8. Morin, William J., Chairman and CEO of Drake Beam Morin, Inc., from a 1981 television tape on job hunting.
9. Williams, Ralph.
10. Drucker, Peter F. *The Practice of Management.* New York: Harper & Brothers Publishers, 3.
11. Schoen, Sterling H., and Douglas E. Durand. *Supervision—The Management of Organizational Resources.* Englewood Cliffs, NJ: Prentice Hall, Inc., 1979, 39.
12. Ibid, preface.
13. Cascio, Dr. Wayne. From an article to be published in 1989 by ASPA/BNA on the structure, mission, and goals of personnel.
14. Sweet, Donald H. *DEcruitment and Outplacement.* Reading, MA: Addison-Wesley Publishing Company, 1975, 10.
15. Peters, Thomas J. and Nancy Austin. *A Passion for Excellence—The Leadership Distance.* New York: Random House, 1985, 63.
16. Brennan, John. *The Conscious Communicator.* Reading, MA: Addison-Wesley Publishing Company, 1974, 3.
17. Ibid, 13.

18. Foulkes, Fred K., *Personnel Policies in Large Non-Union Companies*. Englewood Cliffs, NJ: Prentice-Hall, Inc., 1980, 85286.

19. Seaver, Douglas F., Esq., Chairman, Employment Law Group, Gaston Snow & Ely Bartlett, *Employment Law Bulletin*. Boston, MA, 1986.

20. Allerton, Donald T. and Dr. Michael Nees, Allerton Heinze Associates. "In Search of the Compatible Candidate—the Role of Chemistry in Recruiting," *Report to Clients*. Chicago, 1982.

21. Ibid.

22. Ibid.

23. Day, Berry, and Howard. "Current Legal Issues in the Workplace," Paper prepared for the Northeast Human Resources Association meeting, November 12, 1986.

24. Grossman, Paul. Paul, Hastings, Janofsky & Walker, Los Angeles.

25. Medley, H. Anthony. *Sweaty Palms*. Berkeley, CA: Ten Speed Press, 1980.

26. Lucht, John. *Rites of Passage at $100,000+*. New York: Viceroy Press, 1988, 304.

27.9 Stewart, Nathaniel. *The Effective Woman Manager*. New York: Wiley & Sons, 1978, 208.

Index

About the Author

Author and lecturer Donald H. Sweet is a Career Management Consultant. He held positions with a number of companies including: Celanese Corp., Arthur D. Little, RCA, and the U.S. Navy Dept. As a lecturer he speaks on employment, careers, and related subjects at industry and association meetings, at university and college campuses, and on TV and radio. He is the author of five other books and his articles have appeared in a variety of publications. He has served as chairman of the New York Employment Council; three-term president of the Employment Management Association; and member of the Personnel Committee of the Boy Scouts of America. A graduate of Gettysburg College Mr. Sweet presently resides in New Bern, North Carolina.